Savory Sensation

Beef, Lamb, and Seafood Delights

By

Margaret S. Newman

OF SHELL FISH.

Lobsters.

The middling-sized ones are preferable to the very large ones; the meat is more delicate; plain boiling in salt and water is all they require, or sea water if it can be obtained; though the dressing of this fish is so very simple you very seldom meet with them boiled to perfection; often they are over done, then they have lost their succulence, and eat tough and thready; but if, on the contrary, they are under done, they are very unwholesome and unpalateable; to avoid this mistake I will here give the proper time to boil them; put a lobster weighing one pound into boiling water and let it boil a quarter of an hour; if the lobster weighs two pounds it will require half an hour, and so on in proportion; this is one of the most useful shell fish employed in cooking, as may be seen by the different receipts for fish.

Crabs.

This is also a very delicate fish; it is boiled in the same manner as a lobster, only allowing five minutes longer to each pound, but small ones are useless; they are usually eaten cold with oil and vinegar; to send them to table, dress the meat in the back shell by mixing the soft part with a few bread-crumbs, seasoning it with a little pepper and salt, and putting it in the centre of the shell; then pick the flesh from the large claw with a fork, and filling up the two ends, separating it from the other with some red spawn, place it upon a dish, surround it with the small claws in a circle, and garnish with parsley.

Muscles.

Though very little in use, the flavour of this fish is very delicious in many sauces; many people are afraid to eat them, but with care there is not the slightest danger if prepared in the following manner: wash them well in several waters, and be particular in taking off all the threads that hang to the joints of the shell, put them in a stewpan with two onions (sliced), four cloves, two bay-leaves, and a handful of parsley; set them on a brisk fire and cover them over, toss them over now and then, and when they open of themselves they are done; turn them out of the stewpan, lift off the top shells and take out the fish, beard them and be particular that no small crabs remain in them (as they are supposed to be the unwholesome part), put them in a basin, strain their own liquor over them, and put them by for use. In July and August these fish may be omitted.

Oysters.

The English green oysters are the best that are known; the latter end of August is about the time an epicure would begin to eat them; the small ones are the best for table, and the large ones for culinary purposes; to blanch them open them with care, and put them in a stewpan with their own liquor; let them set, but they must not boil; beard them, strain their own liquor over them in a basin, put them by and use where described.

Pike roasted.

This fish in France is found daily upon the tables of the first epicures, but the quality of this fish there appears much more delicate than here. But perhaps the reason of its being more in vogue there is, that other fish are more scarce; not being so much in use here, (that is, in London,) but in the country, where gentlemen have sport in catching them, they are much more thought of, and to them, perhaps, the following receipts may be the most valuable. To dress it plain it is usually baked, as follows: having well cleaned the fish stuff it with the stuffing for fish   and sew the belly up with packthread; butter a sauté-pan, put the fish into it and place it in the oven for an hour or more, according to the size of it; when done dish it without a napkin and pour anchovy sauce round it; this fish, previous to its being baked, must be trussed with its tail in its mouth, four incisions cut on each side, and well buttered over.

Pike à la Chambord.

The large fish are the only ones fit for this dish (which is much thought of in France). Have the fish well cleaned, and lard it in a square on one side with bacon, put it in a fish-kettle, the larded side upwards, and prepare the following marinade: slice four onions, one carrot, and one turnip, and put them in a stewpan with six bay-leaves, six cloves, two blades of mace, a little thyme, basil, a bunch of parsley, half a pound of lean ham, and half a pound of butter; pass it over a slow fire twenty minutes, keeping it stirred; then add half a bottle of Madeira wine, a wineglassful of vinegar, and six quarts of broth; boil altogether an hour, then pass it through a sieve and pour the liquor into the kettle over the fish; set the fish on the fire to stew for an hour or more, according to the size, but take care the marinade does not cover the fish, moisten the larded part now and then with the stock, and put some burning charcoal on the lid of the kettle; when done glaze it lightly, dish it without a napkin, and have ready the following sauce: put a pint of the stock your fish was stewed in (having previously taken off all the fat) into a stewpan, with two glasses of Madeira wine, reduce it to half, then add two quarts of brown sauce   keep it stirred over the fire till the sauce adheres to the back of the wooden spoon, then add the roes of four carp or mackarel (cut in large pieces, but be careful not to break them), twenty heads of very white mushrooms, twenty cockscombs, twelve large quenelles of whiting   and finish with a tablespoonful of essence of anchovies and half a one of sugar, pour the sauce round the fish, arranging the garniture with taste, add twelve crawfish to the garniture, having previously taken off all the small claws; serve very hot.

This dish I dare say will be but seldom made in this country, on account of its complication, but I thought proper to give it on account of the high estimation in which it is held in France; I must however observe that I have omitted some of the garniture which would make it still more expensive, and if there should be any difficulty in getting what remains, the sauce is very good without.

Pike en matelote.

Stuff and bake the fish as before; when done, dress it without a napkin, and pour a sauce matelote (see Saumon en matelote marinière,   in the middle and round the fish, and serve very hot. Or the fish may be stewed as in the last.

Pike à la Hollandaise.

Boil the fish in salt and water, in the same manner as cod-fish; drain it well, dish it without a napkin, pour a sauce Hollandaise over it. (For sauce, see Turbot à la Hollandaise,

Small Pike à la Meunière.

Crimp a small pike, it must not weigh more than two pounds, but smaller if you can get it, and proceed exactly as for Sole à la meunière
but allow it more time.

Pike with caper sauce.

Boil the fish as before, and have ready caper sauce made as follows: put fifteen tablespoonfuls of melted butter in a stewpan, and when it boils add a quarter of a pound of fresh butter; when it melts, add two tablespoonfuls of liaison   let it remain on the fire to thicken, but do not let it boil; moisten with a little milk if required, then add two tablespoonfuls of capers, and pour over the fish.

Pike à la Maître d'Hôtel.

Boil the fish as usual, and dish it without a napkin; then put twelve tablespoonfuls of melted butter in a stewpan; and when it is upon the point of boiling, add a quarter of a pound of maître d'hôtel butter, and when it melts pour over and round the fish; serve very hot.

Pike à l'Egyptienne.

Cut two onions, two turnips, one carrot, one head of celery, and one leek into slices; put them into a large stewpan with some parsley, thyme, bay-leaves, and a pint of port wine; then have your fish ready trussed, with its tail in its mouth; put it into the stewpan, with the vegetables; add three pints of broth, and set it on a slow fire to stew, with some live charcoal upon the lid; try, when done, by running the knife close in to the back bone; if the meat detaches easily, it is done; take it out, and place on a baking sheet; dry it with a cloth, then egg and bread-crumb it; put it in the oven, and salamander it a light brown; then put twenty tablespoonfuls of white sauce   in a stewpan, with eight of milk, and reduce it five minutes; then add four gherkins, the whites of four hard-boiled eggs, and two truffles, cut in very small dice; finish with two tablespoonfuls of essence of anchovies, the juice of half a lemon, and four pats of butter; dress the fish without a napkin, and sauce over.

Fillets of Pike à la Maître d'Hôtel.

Fillet three small pike and dress them in the manner described in Fillets of mackerel à la Vénitienne   dress them round on a dish without a napkin, and sauce over with the same sauce as Pike à la maître d'hôtel.

Fillets of Pike en matelote.

If for a dinner for twelve, fillet four small pike; egg and bread-crumb, and fry in oil; dish them round on a border of mashed potatoes (previously cutting each fillet in halves) and serve sauce matelote in the centre.

Fillets of Pike à la Meunière.

Fillet four pike as above, cut each fillet in halves, rub some chopped eschalot into them, dip them in flour, broil them; when done, sauce as for Sole à la meunière Observe, if you happen to live in the country where pike is plentiful, you may dish the fillets in as many ways as soles or any other fish; but I have omitted giving them here, thinking it useless to fill a useful book with so many repetitions; we have several ways of dressing pike to be eaten cold in France, which I have also omitted, as they would be quite useless in this country.

Carp en matelote.

Have your fish ready cleaned, and make four or five incisions on each side; then put two sliced onions, three sprigs of thyme and parsley, and half a pint of port wine in a stewpan, or small fish-kettle; season the fish with pepper and salt, lay it in the stewpan, add four pints of broth, and place it on a slow fire to stew for an hour (which will be sufficient for a fish of five pounds weight), or more in proportion to the size; when done, dress it on a dish, without a napkin; drain it well, and serve a matelote sauce
over it, only use some of the stock from the fish (having previously taken off all the fat) instead of plain broth, as directed in that article.

Carp à la Genoise.

Prepare your fish as above, and lay it in your fish-kettle, with two ounces of salt, half a bottle of port wine, two onions, two turnips, one leek, one carrot (cut in slices), three bay-leaves, six cloves, two blades of mace, and a sprig of parsley, cover the fish with white broth; stew it as before, dress it without a napkin, prepare a sauce Genoise and pour over it.

Stewed Carp à la Marquise.

Cook the fish as above, and when done, dress it on a dish without a napkin, and have ready the following sauce: put twenty tablespoonfuls of white sauce in a stewpan, reduce it over a fire until rather thick, then add a gill of whipt cream, two tablespoonfuls of capers, and two of chopped gherkins; pour over the fish, then sprinkle two tablespoonfuls of chopped beet-root over it, and serve.

Carp with caper sauce.

Cook the fish as above, and dress it without a napkin; then put twenty-five tablespoonfuls of melted butter into a stewpan, and when nearly boiling add a quarter of a pound of fresh butter; stir it till the butter melts, then add four tablespoonfuls of capers, and pour over. This sauce must be rather thick.

Carp fried.

Open the fish down the back with a sharp knife from the head to the tail, cutting off half the head, so that the fish is quite flat; break the backbone in three places, but allow the roe to remain; then dip the fish in flour, and fry it in hot lard; dress it on a napkin, garnish with parsley, and serve plain melted butter, well seasoned, in a boat.

Tench en matelote.

This fish, though not much thought of by our first-rate epicures, is, according to my opinion, superior to carp; in a matelote it is excellent.

Have your fish prepared for cooking, and put them into a small fish-kettle (with a drainer); and if two middle-sized fish, put two onions, half a carrot, one turnip, three bay-leaves, a bunch of parsley, four cloves, a blade of mace, ten allspice, half a pint of port wine, and half a pint of broth in the kettle with them; place them over a moderate fire, stew them half an hour, or more if required; when done drain them well; dress without a napkin, and pour a matelote sauce

Tench à la Poulette.

Stew the fish as before, only use bucellas instead of port wine; then peel thirty button onions, pass them in a stewpan (over a fire) with a little powdered sugar and butter till they are covered with a white glaze; then add two glasses of bucellas wine, boil it three minutes; then put twenty tablespoonfuls of white sauce, and ten of the stock from the fish in with it, and let it simmer on the corner of the fire till the onions are quite done, keeping it well skimmed; then season with a little pepper, salt, and sugar, and add twenty muscles (blanched), a little chopped parsley, and a tablespoonful of lemon-juice; take it off the fire, stir in four tablespoonfuls of liaison, and pour over the fish; serve very hot. The sauce requires to be thick enough to well cover the fish.

Tench sauce aux Moules.

Stew the fish as before, dish it up without a napkin, have ready a muscle sauce   pour it over the fish, and serve very hot.

Tench fried or broiled.

Is very good served with anchovy or shrimp sauce in a boat.

Perch à la Hollandaise.

Have three middling-sized fishes ready prepared for cooking; then put two ounces of butter, two onions (in slices), one carrot (cut small), some parsley, two bay-leaves, six cloves, and two blades of mace in a stewpan; pass it five minutes over a brisk fire, then add a quart of water, two glasses of vinegar, one ounce of salt, and a little pepper; boil altogether a quarter of an hour, and pass it through a sieve into a small fish-kettle; then lay the fishes into it, and let them stew twenty or thirty minutes over a moderate fire; dress them on a dish without a napkin, and pour a sauce Hollandaise

Perch à la Maître d'Hôtel

Prepare and cook your fish as above; then put twenty tablespoonfuls of melted butter in a stewpan, and when it is upon the point of boiling, add a quarter of a pound of Maître d'Hôtel butter   and pour the sauce over the fish, which dress on a dish without a napkin.

Small Perches en water souchet.

Cut four small fishes in halves, having previously taken off all the scales, and proceed precisely as for Flounders en water souchet

Small Perches frits au beurre.

Scale and well dry six perches, and make incisions here and there on each side of them; then put a quarter of a pound of butter into a sauté-pan, season your fishes with pepper and salt, put them in the sauté-pan and fry them gently, turning them carefully; when done, dress them on a napkin, garnish with parsley, and serve without sauce.

In my opinion, they are much better cooked this way than boiled or stewed; large fish may also be done this way, but they require more butter, and must cook very slowly.

Trout plain boiled.

Trout that is caught in a river or running stream is preferable to that caught in a lake or pond; although I have had very fine ones from ponds, they have invariably tasted muddy; in fact a running stream is better for all fish in this respect; but still water most affects the flavour of the trout.

Prepare the fish for cooking, and boil it in salt and water; if it weighs two pounds, allow it half an hour, and more in proportion; dress it on a napkin, garnish with parsley, and serve shrimp-sauce in a boat.

Trout à la Maître d'Hôtel.

Stew the fish like perch, allowing more time in proportion to the size; dress them on a dish without a napkin, and sauce the same as Perche à la Maître d'Hôtel

Trout à la Genoise.

Stew the fish as above, dress it on a dish without a napkin, and pour a sauce Genoise

Trout à la Beyrout.

Dry your fish with a cloth, flour it, and lay it on the gridiron; broil it nicely over a moderate fire; when done, peel off all the skin; dish it without a napkin, and pour a sauce Beyrout

Fillets of Trout à la Mazarine.

Fillet a fish, and cut each fillet in halves; fry it in butter, like perch, dress it round on a dish, and pour a sauce Mazarine over them. For sauce, see Turbot à la Mazarine,   or they may be served with a matelote sauce in change.

Eels fried.

Cut the eels in pieces about three inches long, dip them in flour, egg and bread-crumb, and fry them in very hot lard, dress them on a napkin, garnish with parsley, and serve shrimp-sauce in a boat.

Eels à la Tartare.

Cut the eels and fry as above, have ready some Tartare sauce upon a cold dish, lay the eels upon it and serve immediately; should the eels be large they must be three parts stewed before they are fried; dry them upon a cloth previous to bread-crumbing them.

Spitchcocked Eels.

Take the bones out of the eels by opening them from head to tail, and cut them in pieces about four inches long, throw them into some flour, then have ready upon a dish about a couple of handfuls of bread-crumbs, a tablespoonful of chopped parsley, a little dried thyme, and a little cayenne pepper, then egg each piece of eel and bread-crumb them with it, fry them in very hot lard, dish them on a napkin, and serve shrimp-sauce in a boat.

Stewed Eels.

Cut the eels in pieces as before, and tie each piece round with packthread, then put them into a stewpan with an onion, a tablespoonful of white wine, three cloves, three whole allspice, a bunch of parsley, thyme, and bay-leaf, and a little white broth, sufficient to cover them; place them over a moderate fire, and let them stew gently for half an hour or more, if required, (according to the size of the eel,) take them out, drain them on a napkin, dish them without a napkin, and have ready the following sauce: put a teaspoonful of chopped onions into a stewpan with four tablespoonfuls of white wine, and eight ditto of brown sauce   let it boil gently for a quarter of an hour, keeping it stirred, then add a teaspoonful of essence of anchovies and a little sugar, and pour over your eels.

Eels en matelote.

Stew the eels as above, dress them without a napkin, and pour a sauce matelote   over them. They may also be served with a sauce à la Beyrout

Lampreys.

Are fish not so often used as eels, though they are remarkably good eating; but I think they have got out of repute by being so often served underdone; they may be stewed in the same manner as eels, (only a lamprey requires double the time stewing that an eel of the same size would require), and serve with the same sauces, with matelote sauce especially; if you fry or broil them they must be three parts boiled beforehand; to try when done run a trussing needle into them, if it goes in easy they are done.

Crawfish.

These are very favourite little shell-fish, and much used in France, but seldom served as a dish in this country (they are not good when in spawn); for a dish have two dozen of them and wash in several waters (choose them as near as possible of equal sizes), then put them in a stewpan, with two onions, one carrot, one turnip, one head of celery, six bay-leaves, a bunch of parsley, six cloves, twelve peppercorns, half an ounce of salt, half a teaspoonful of pepper, a quarter ditto of cayenne, two glasses of vinegar, four of sherry, and half a pint of broth; place them over a very brisk fire for twenty-five minutes, stirring them occasionally, take them off the fire and let them cool in their stock, put them in a basin, cover them with the stock, but strain the vegetables away from them, and use for garnishing where directed; to make a dish dress them on butter in the form of a bush, mingling very green double parsley with them.

HORS-D'ŒUVRES, OR DISHES TO BE HANDED ROUND THE TABLE.

Petits Vol-au-Vents à la Moëlle de Bœuf.

Make a pound of puff paste roll it half an inch in thickness, then cut out your vol-au-vents with a fluted cutter rather larger than a five-shilling piece; have ready a baking sheet, (on which you have sprinkled some water,) and put your vol-au-vents on it, egg them over with a paste brush, and cut a top with a small plain cutter, which is done by dipping the cutter into hot water, and just marking a ring upon the top of each vol-au-vent, but do not cut it deep, then put them in a very warm oven, and pay particular attention to the baking of them, which will occupy about twenty minutes, keep the oven door shut as much as possible, take them out when done, and with the point of a knife take off the lid without breaking it, and take out the soft paste remaining inside, leaving them quite empty, they are then ready for immediate use; prepare the marrow as follows: take all the marrow from a beef marrow-bone, in as large pieces as possible, have ready on the fire a stewpan of boiling water, into which throw the marrow, and let it boil ten minutes, then take it out carefully and put it in cold water, put a pint of brown sauce into a stewpan, with four spoonfuls of brown gravy and a small piece of glaze, and reduce it till it becomes rather thick, then cut the marrow in dice about a quarter of an inch square, and two minutes before serving throw it into the sauce, with two large quenelles also cut in dice, whilst boiling, previously draining them upon a cloth; warm it quickly, season with a little salt and sugar if required, fill the vol-au-vents, and dress them on a napkin pyramidically; serve very hot.

Petits Vol-au-Vents au laitance de Maquereau.

Make the vol-au-vents as in the previous article, put two ounces of butter into a sauté-pan, rub it over the bottom, have ready four soft roes of mackerel, then put into the sauté-pan with a little pepper, salt, chopped parsley, and a teaspoonful of lemon-juice; set them over a moderate fire five minutes, turn them, and when done cut them in small dice, but let them remain in the sauté-pan, then add eight tablespoonfuls of white sauce and two of light broth, a little sugar, and two or three tablespoonfuls of cream; stir it over the fire and mix it well without breaking the roes, fill your vol-au-vents, and serve very hot on a napkin; carp roes may be served in the same manner.

Petits Vol-au-Vents au foie de Raie.

Make the vol-au-vents as above; boil the liver of a skate in salt and water an hour, let it get cold, put six tablespoonfuls of white sauce in a stewpan, with four of light stock, and reduce it till rather thick, then add a little chopped parsley, three tablespoonfuls of cream, a little white pepper, sugar, and salt, if required; cut the liver in small dice, with four quenelles put it in the stewpan, make it hot, but do not stir it much or you will break it, add a little lemon-juice, fill the vol-au-vents, and serve as before. These patties, although seldom served, are very excellent if well done and nicely seasoned.

Petits Vol-au-Vents aux Huîtres.

Prepare the vol-au-vents as before, put eight tablespoonfuls of white sauce in a stewpan, with a little cayenne pepper, a teaspoonful of essence of anchovies, two peppercorns, half a blade of mace, and six tablespoonfuls of liquor from the oysters, reduce it till very thick, have ready, blanched and bearded, two dozen oysters cut each oyster in four pieces, put them in the sauce, (previously taking out the peppercorns and mace,) with a little salt, sugar, and lemon-juice, make it hot over the fire, add a little cream, but do not let it boil, or the oysters would become tough and the sauce very thin: fill the vol-au-vents and serve on a napkin as before.

Petits Vol-au-Vents de Homard.

Prepare the vol-au-vents as usual, put eight tablespoonfuls of white sauce and four of light stock, in a stewpan, with a little cayenne pepper, salt, and a teaspoonful of essence of anchovies, boil it ten minutes, then cut a small hen lobster up in large dice, pound the red spawn from it with one ounce of butter, pass it through a hair sieve and mix with the sauce; put in the lobster, make it hot, fill your vol-au-vent, and serve as before.

N. B. The last four dishes may be made maigre by substituting melted butter or oyster sauce for white sauce.

Petites Bouchées à la Moëlle de Bœuf.

Are made in the same manner as the petits vol-au-vents, but the paste must not be more than a quarter of an inch in thickness, and the bouchées must be cut with a fluted cutter not larger than half-a-crown piece, bake them in a warmer oven than the vol-au-vents, prepare the beef marrow, fill and serve the same as

Petites Bouchées au laitance de Maquereau.

Make the bouchées as before, and prepare the mackerel roes the same as for petits vol-au-vents

Petites Bouchées à la Reine.

Prepare them as usual, pick the meat of the half of a braised chicken, and cut it in very small dice (not larger than peas), cut about the same size one ounce of cooked tongue, six blanched mushrooms, and two middling-sized French truffles; mix altogether, then put twenty tablespoonfuls of white sauce in a stewpan, with eight of milk, reduce it to one half, then add the minced fowl, tongue, &c., season with a little lemon-juice, pepper, salt, sugar, and two spoonfuls of cream; serve them very hot on a napkin.

Petites Bouchées à la purée de Volaille.

Prepare them as before, take about half a pound of the flesh of chicken, turkey, or any description of poultry; pound it well in a mortar, with half an ounce of lean boiled ham, then put a teaspoonful of chopped eschalots in a stewpan, with half an ounce of butter, pass them over the fire, stirring them with a wooden spoon, then add a little flour, mix it well with the butter and eschalots, then add the pounded meat, four spoonfuls of white sauce, and half a pint of good stock that the bones of the poultry have been previously boiled in, boil altogether a quarter of an hour, season with a little white pepper, salt, and sugar, pass it through a tammie by rubbing it with two wooden spoons, put it into another stewpan, boil it, finish with a tablespoonful of liaison, fill the bouchées, and serve on a napkin very hot.

Petites Bouchées de Gibier.

Prepare the bouchées as before, put twenty tablespoonfuls of game sauce in a stewpan, then cut up into small dice the flesh of a grouse, partridge, half a pheasant, or the remains of any game you might happen to have by you, put it in the stewpan with the sauce, make it hot but do not let it boil, season with a little sugar and salt, fill and serve as before.

Petites Bouchées à la purée de Gibier.

Prepare them as before, and proceed as for the petites bouchées à la purée de volaille, only using the flesh of game, and game sauce, instead of the flesh of poultry and white sauce.

Petits Pâtés à la Pâtissière.

Make one pound of puff paste roll it into a sheet a quarter of an inch in thickness, then cut twenty pieces of the size of a five-shilling piece with a plain round cutter; mix the remains of the paste together, and roll them out to the thickness of the eighth of an inch, and cut twenty more pieces from it with the same cutter, sprinkle a baking sheet with water and lay them on it a little distance apart, wash them over with a little water with a paste brush, then have ready prepared in a basin half a pound of forcemeat of veal, fowl, or game with which mix half an ounce of beef marrow chopped very fine, one eschalot, a little parsley also chopped fine, and the yolk of an egg; mix well together with a wooden spoon, then put a little lump of the forcemeat half the size of a walnut on each piece of paste on the baking sheet, cover them over with the twenty pieces of paste you first cut, and close them well at the edges by pressing them down with the top part of a smaller cutter, egg the tops over, but be careful that the egg does not run down the sides, or it would prevent the patties from rising straight, put them in rather a hot oven and bake them about twenty minutes; dish them in pyramid on a napkin and serve; to be good they should be served directly they are taken from the oven; care should be taken not to put too much forcemeat in them, or it will upset them in baking.

Rissoles aux Huîtres.

Put half a tablespoonful of chopped onions into a stewpan, with half an ounce of butter, place it over the fire, fry the onions, but they must be kept white; then add half a teaspoonful of flour, and twelve of oyster liquor, (mix well) and eight tablespoonfuls of white sauce   boil altogether ten minutes (or more till it becomes rather thickish), keeping it stirred the whole time, season with a little cayenne pepper, and salt, (it requires to be seasoned rather high,) then have ready blanched three dozen of oysters, cut each into four pieces, dry them on a cloth, and put them into the sauce, let them boil two minutes, add a few drops of essence of anchovies, and three yolks of eggs,stir again over the fire a minute to set the eggs, then put it out on a dish and set it to get cold; make half a pound of puff paste
roll it ten times, (or the trimmings of paste previously made will do,) roll it out as thin as a shilling, then cut it out with a round cutter the size of the top of a small teacup, lay a teaspoonful of the preparation of oyster on each piece, wet it round with the paste brush, turn one edge over on to the other and close it well, then egg and bread-crumb them, fry in very hot lard (enough for them to swim in), when done dish them on a napkin, garnish with fried parsley and serve very hot; it will take about five minutes to fry them.

Rissoles de Homard.

Put a teaspoonful of chopped onions into a stewpan with half an ounce of fresh butter, fry them white, then add ten or fifteen tablespoonfuls of white sauce (according to the size of the lobster), stir over the fire and let it boil five minutes, or more, until rather thick, have a fresh lobster cut up into small dice, put it into the sauce, season with cayenne pepper, salt, a little chopped parsley, juice of a lemon, and a few drops of essence of anchovies, let it boil a minute, then add two yolks of eggs, stir it over the fire another minute, to set the eggs, and pour it out on a dish to get cold; make and serve the rissoles as in the last article.

Rissoles of Shrimps.

Prepare the salpicon exactly the same as the lobster in the last article, but be careful that the shrimps are not too salt; prawns are better for this purpose than shrimps; they require but very little seasoning; make, fry, and serve the rissoles as before.

Rissoles de laitances de Maquereau.

Put a quarter of a pound of butter in a sauté-pan, rub it over the bottom, lay in the soft roes of four mackerel, season them with a little white pepper, salt, a teaspoonful of lemon-juice, and a very little chopped parsley; place them over a moderate fire five minutes, turn them, but do not let them get the least brown; when quite done cut them into small dice without breaking, then put half a teaspoonful of chopped eschalots into a stewpan, with a few drops of salad oil; fry them quite white, then mix half a teaspoonful of flour with them, and ten tablespoonfuls of white sauce   stir it over the fire, and boil till it becomes very thick (as the roes of mackerel are so very delicate), season with a little cayenne pepper, salt, and a little sugar if required; then put in two yolks of eggs, mix well, and add the mackerel roes, stir it very gently over the fire till the eggs become set, then put it on a dish to get cold; make, dress, and serve the rissoles as before. This delicate hors-d'œuvre requires great attention and proper seasoning.

Rissoles de Gibier.

Roast a grouse or any other bird rather underdone, or the remains of some game left from a previous dinner will do, pick the meat off the bones and cut it into very small dice; then put a teaspoonful of chopped eschalots in a stewpan, with a quarter of an ounce of butter, fry them rather brown, add ten tablespoonfuls of game sauce (if none, make some with the bones as directed,   and four of brown ditto   reduce over the fire till it becomes rather thick, season with a little cayenne pepper, salt, a teaspoonful of chopped mushrooms, and a teaspoonful of wine; let it boil, then add the game, with a little sugar and two yolks of eggs, stir it gently over the fire just to set the eggs, pour it on a dish to cool; make, dress, and serve the rissoles as before.

Rissoles de Volaille.

Cut half a roast (or boiled) fowl up into very small dice, then put a teaspoonful of chopped eschalots in a stewpan, with half an ounce of butter, fry them quite white, then add sixteen tablespoonfuls of white sauce
put it over the fire to reduce till it is rather thick, put the fowl into the sauce, season with a little salt, white pepper, sugar, a teaspoonful of chopped mushrooms, and a little chopped parsley; let it boil a few minutes, then stir in the yolks of two eggs, let them set, and pour it on a dish to cool (a little ham or tongue may be mixed with the above, if required;) make, fry, and serve the rissoles as before.

Rissoles may also be made of turkey, pigeons, veal, lamb, sweetbread, &c., by following the above receipt, and using either one or the other of those articles instead of fowl.

Croustade de Beurre.

Have ready a lump of fresh butter very hard and cut it into slices one inch and a half in thickness, lay them upon a table or slab in a cool place; then take a round cutter the size of half-a-crown, and with it cut twelve pieces of the butter out of the slices, beat up three or four eggs on a plate, put the pieces of butter into them, then take them out and throw them into a dish of bread-crumbs, take them out, throw them again into the eggs, and then the bread-crumbs, repeating the process three times, lay them upright upon the table, and mark a ring a little larger than a shilling on the top of each with a smaller cutter, stand them in a wire basket and fry in very hot lard, of a nice light-brown colour, and very crisp, take them out, take off the lids, empty them with care, and you will save nearly all the butter from them, turn them topsy-turvey in a dry place until wanted; when ready to serve put them in the oven a short time to get hot, and fill with any of the preparations for petites bouchées. You may form the croustades in diamonds, or any shape your fancy dictates; they make very beautiful hors-d'œuvres, and very cheap, as with care you may save the butter, which when cold may be applied to any other purpose.

Croustade de Beurre à la Duke of York.

Prépare the croustades as above, and make a good purée of fowl (as for petites bouchées à la purée de volaille,   then peel a good sized cucumber, cut it in pieces two inches long, and divide each piece into three lengthwise, take out the seeds, and stew the pieces of cucumber till very tender, with a little sugar, onion, and broth, keeping them very white; when cold cut them in small dice, mix with the purée of fowl, fill the croustades, and serve very hot with a plover's egg upon the top of each.

Croquettes de Homard.

Prepare a salpicon of lobster the same as for rissoles de homard; when quite cold cut it out in pieces two inches long and three quarters of an inch wide, beat up three or four eggs on a plate, and throw each piece into them and then into a dish of bread-crumbs, take them out, roll them lightly with the hand, beat them gently with a knife to make the crumbs stick, then throw them again into the eggs and bread-crumb, smooth them again with a knife, fry in hot lard, and dress them on a napkin garnished with fried parsley; they may be made in the form of pears or any way that fancy dictates, giving them the shape previous to bread-crumbing them. Croquettes may be made of any of the preparations for rissoles by following the above direction.

Aiguillettes de Ris de Veau.

For these kind of hors-d'œuvres it is necessary to have twelve small silver skewers, about four inches long and the thickness of a packing-needle, with a ring or fancy design on the top, they are not very expensive but are very novel for this description of dishes; the persons eating what is served upon them taking the head of the skewer with the fingers of their left hand and picking it off with their fork. Boil three throat sweetbreads in water ten minutes, pour off the water and add one onion, one carrot, one turnip, two bay-leaves, and a pint of white broth, let them simmer about twenty minutes till firm, then take them out of the broth, lay them on a clean cloth, cut them in pieces, with a long round cutter, about the size of a shilling, and season with pepper and salt; then chop two eschalots very fine and put them in a stewpan with an ounce of butter; fry them quite white, add ten tablespoonfuls of white sauce   and eight of light stock, reduce until rather thick, add two yolks of eggs and the juice of half a lemon, take it off the fire, but do not let it boil after the yolks of eggs are in, then dip each piece of sweetbread into the sauce with a fork, and lay them on a dish till cold, then run the skewers through the centre of each piece, putting two pieces on each skewer, have ready four eggs well beaten on a plate, dip each skewer into the eggs and then into the bread-crumbs twice over, fry in hot lard, and serve them very hot on a napkin.

Aiguillettes (escalopes) aux Huîtres.

Put eighteen tablespoonfuls of good oyster sauce into a stewpan, reduce it until rather thick, then add two yolks of eggs, stir them well in, and take it off the fire; choose rather small oysters, have them ready blanched and bearded, dip them one by one into the sauce with a fork, and lay them on a dish to cool; when quite cold run the skewers through (placing five on each skewer), dip them in eggs and bread-crumbs twice over as before, fry them in hot lard, and serve very hot on a napkin.

Aiguillettes (escalopes) de Homard.

Cut forty pieces of lobster the size round of a shilling, and one inch in thickness, then put a teaspoonful of chopped eschalots in a stewpan, with a very small piece of butter, fry them quite white, then add eight tablespoonfuls of oyster sauce reduce till rather thick, season with a little sugar, cayenne, and the juice of half a lemon, finish with the yolks of two eggs, dip the pieces of lobster into it and proceed as before; fry, dish, and serve in the same manner; the onions may be avoided if objectionable.

Aiguillettes de filets de Sole.

Fillet a sole, butter a sauté-pan, lay in the fillets, season with pepper, salt, and the juice of a lemon, place them over a slow fire and when done lay them flat on a dish, place another dish on them, upon which put a four pounds weight, when cold cut them in pieces with a cutter the size of a shilling, prepare oyster sauce as above, dip each piece in the sauce and proceed exactly as before.

Aiguillettes aux Huîtres.

Make a preparation of oysters the same as for rissoles aux huîtres, adding one more yolk of egg; when cold make thin croquettes two inches long, egg and bread-crumb them once, pass a silver skewer through each, then egg and bread-crumb again, fry and serve on a napkin with fried parsley.

Aiguillettes de Homard.

Make the preparation as for croquettes de homard and proceed exactly as in the last.

Aiguillettes de Sole.

Make a preparation as for croquettes de homard, only using the fillets of soles instead of lobster, and proceed as before.

Aiguilettes de Volaille à la jolie fille.

Make a preparation as for rissoles de volaille but adding tongue, truffles, and pistachios cut in small fillets; when cold make them into croquettes about two inches long, but do not bread-crumb them; pass a silver skewer through, then have ready some batter for frying
hold each skewer by the head, pour some batter over each croquette with a spoon, covering every part of them, and fry in lard, but not too hot, as they must be quite white and crisp; dress them on a napkin and serve very hot.

For Aiguilettes de Gibier à la jolie fille proceed exactly as above, only using game in the preparation instead of fowl.

In France hors-d'œuvres are made of tastefully dressed anchovy salads, olives, &c., to invigorate the appetite, which is unrequired at this almost the commencement of the dinner.

REMOVES.

Croustades of Bread for removes.

Although it is against my principle to have any unnecessary ornamental work in a dinner, I am rather partial to these croustades, they being simple and very elegant. It would be quite useless my attempting to explain by receipts the manner in which they are made, as so much depends upon the taste and skill of the artist. Having invented several new removes requiring croustades of different designs, I have had them engraved, and think I may say that the whole of the designs there represented are quite original. These croustades are cut out of one or two loaves of bread; when cut in separate pieces they are joined by running a silver skewer (or attelet) through them; the body of the croustades is fried in lard, of a nice straw-colour, and the small ornaments attached are cut with cutters and fried in oil, some must be kept quite white and others allowed to get very black; they are fixed to the body of the croustade with a stiffish paste made of whites of eggs and flour; my reason for departing from the old-fashioned custom of placing them in the centre of a dish and putting them at the head, is that it facilitates the carving, and you are not so subject to get pieces of it in your plate with the sauce, besides which I think it has a more novel appearance, and makes the dish more elegant.

To obtain, lard, and dress a filet of Beef.

A fillet of beef can only be procured in this country by purchasing a rump and sirloin together, (in France it is sold as a separate joint,) but the rump and sirloin can be used for other dishes, or for the servants' meals, and in families where they kill their own meat, it is of no consequence. To cut out the fillet lay the rump and sirloin upon the table, the inside uppermost, then pass your knife along close to the chine bone, keeping the knife close to the bone until you get past the fillet, then commence cutting upwards through the fat, which trim from the fillet, except a little at the sides, then with a sharp knife take all the skin from the top of the fillet, beat it lightly, and lard it nicely lengthwise with small lardons of fat bacon, two inches in length, and the thickness of a quill; have prepared and cut in slices six onions, two carrots, two turnips, one head of celery, one leek, a handful of parsley, a few sprigs of thyme, and six bay-leaves, moisten with a teacupful of salad oil, lay your fillet on a large dish and cover with the vegetables, let it remain thus all night; to cook it run a lark spit through the length of the fillet, lay all the vegetables upon four sheets of paper, (or more, for if not sufficient paper it will burst and the vegetables fall in the dripping-pan,) lay the fillet upon them, cover and tie it up surrounded with the vegetables; baste it well when you first put it to the fire, to prevent the paper from burning, roast an hour and a half or a little longer before a good fire; when done, take it from the vegetables, glaze the larded part, brown lightly with the salamander, and it is ready to be sauced and served. It may also be roasted without the vegetables, but then an hour would suffice.

Fillet of Beef à la Joan d'Arc.

Prepare and cook the fillet as described, then cut a croustade in the form of a breast-plate (see plate), fix it at the head of the dish upon paste, then lay your fillet in the middle of a dish, make a small border of mashed potatoes round, upon which alternately place a small quenelle and a small fillet of tongue, to match; proceed in like manner all the way round, then have ready nicely boiled twenty heads of fine asparagus, cut half of them five inches in length, and the remainder three inches, dress them inside of the croustade on the top to represent arrows, pour a jus d'eschalotte sauce over the fillet, glaze the quenelles and tongue, and serve very hot.

Fillet of Beef à la Beyrout.

Prepare and dress the fillet as before, then cut a croustade of bread representing the wall of a citadel, form the cannons with stewed carrots, and the balls with truffles, place it on mashed potatoes at the head of the dish, lay the fillet in the centre, make a border of mashed potatoes round, rather high, close to the croustade on each side, but diminishing as you go from it; have ready twenty crawfish, place them on the potatoes, tails upwards, pour a sauce Beyrout round the fillet; glaze and serve.

I must here observe that as crawfish are frequently served to garnish calf's head, I see no impropriety in using them to garnish beef.

Fillet of Beef au jus de Tomate.

Prepare and dress the fillet as described above, dish it up plain, pour the sauce au jus de tomate round it; glaze and serve very hot.

Fillet of Beef Napolitaine.

Prepare and dress the fillet as described place it in the centre of the dish, have ready two croustades, the shape and size of scallop shells, fix one at each end of the fillet on mashed potatoes, and fill them with fresh scraped horseradish, then have ready the following sauce: make a mierpoix of two onions, two turnips, one carrot, one apple, a quarter of a pound of lean ham (cut in thin slices), half a clove of garlic, one bay-leaf, and three tablespoonfuls of salad oil; pass the whole twenty minutes over a slow fire (in a stewpan), then add four tablespoonfuls of Tarragon vinegar, boil it five minutes, add a pint and a half of brown sauce and a pint of consommé reduce it to half, skim off all the oil, then add six tablespoonfuls of very red tomate sauce, one ditto of orange marmalade, and two of currant jelly, let it boil a few minutes longer, pass it through a tammie into another stewpan, season rather high, have ready a quarter of a pound of Smyrna raisins (well soaked in water for one hour), and twelve of the best quality French plums cut in quarters lengthwise, throw them into the sauce, make it hot, pour round the beef, which glaze very nicely and serve.

Fillet of Beef à la Strasbourgienne.

Prepare and dress your fillets as directed, adding four glasses of sherry to the vegetables you roast it in; prepare two croustades the size and shape of scallop shells, dress your beef in the middle of the dish, placing a croustade (on mashed potatoes) at each end; have ready previously boiled two pounds of Strasburg bacon (which, from its dry nature requires soaking two days and boiling four hours), cut it in slices two inches long, and have an equal number of sliced of fried potatoes to match, make a border of mashed potatoes round the beef, and dress the slices of bacon and fried potatoes alternately upon it, have ready prepared the following sauce: put a tablespoonful of chopped eschalots in a stewpan, with three of Tarragon vinegar, let it reduce to half, then add a pint and a half of brown sauce, two spoonfuls of tomate sauce a pint of consommé and half a tablespoonful of sugar, let it boil quickly twenty minutes, skim well, and reduce until it adheres to the back of the spoon, then have ready a lemon, peeled, sliced, blanched in boiling water, and drained on a hair sieve, which throw in the sauce, pour it round the beef, fill one of the croustades with stoned French olives, and the other with Indian pickle made hot in a little demi-glace

Fillet of Beef à la Napolitaine.

Prepare and dress the fillet as directed dress it plain on a dish and have ready prepared the following sauce: cut in thin slices two onions, half a carrot, one turnip, half a head of celery, two bay-leaves, a sprig of thyme, a bunch of parsley, three cloves, one blade of mace, and a quarter of a pound of lean ham; put them into a stewpan with two ounces of butter, stir it over a brisk fire till getting rather brown at the bottom, then add four tablespoonfuls of tarragon vinegar, let it reduce to half, then add a quart of brown sauce and a pint of consommé stir it until boiling, then place it at the corner of the stove to simmer a quarter of an hour, skim it, then add a tablespoonful of chopped mushrooms, a little grated horseradish, and three tablespoonfuls of currant jelly; boil it quickly five minutes, and pass it through a tammie into a clean stewpan, add a quarter of a pound of Smyrna raisins well washed and soaked, pour the sauce over the beef, garnish with scraped horseradish and hard-boiled eggs cut in quarters lengthwise and laid near the rim of the dish.

Fillet of Beef à la Milanaise.

Prepare and lard the fillet as before, then make a stiffish paste of flour and water, roll it about half an inch in thickness and fold the fillet in it, fold it again in three sheets of paper, tie it up at both ends, run a lark spit through it, and just as you are going to put it down to roast open the paste, pour in three glasses of Madeira wine, close the paste well, tie it up securely, roast it two hours, take it up and remove from the paste, glaze it, brown lightly with the salamander, dish it plain, and have ready the following sauce: cut half a pound of blanched maccaroni into pieces an inch long, likewise two ounces of very red cooked tongue, six large blanched mushrooms, and four middling-sized French truffles, put twenty spoonfuls of white sauce
in a stewpan, stir it over the fire five minutes, season with half a teaspoonful of salt, a small quantity of cayenne, and a little sugar, add all the other ingredients, with half a pound of grated Parmesan, stir the whole

over the fire to get hot, but do not break the pieces; moisten with a little cream, pour the sauce in the dish, lay the fillet upon it, glaze and serve.

Fillet of Beef à la Bohémienne.

Trim and lard a fillet as directed, cut in thin slices six onions, two carrots, three turnips, three heads of celery, and a leek; put them into a dish large enough to hold the fillet, then put a quart of vinegar into a stewpan, with a pint of broth; when it boils put in a few peppercorns, nine cloves, two blades of mace, four bay-leaves, a sprig of thyme and sweet marjoram, a small bunch of parsley, half a pound of brown sugar, and a little salt, let it boil twenty minutes and pour it over the vegetables; when it gets cold lay in the fillet of beef, covering it over with the vegetables, let it remain in this pickle six days, turning it every day; when ready to cook roast it in paste as in the previous article, brown it with the salamander, serve it in the middle of the dish, make a low border of mashed potatoes round it, have ready potatoes fried (and cut in slices in the shape of cotelettes) dish them upon the border of mashed potatoes round the beef, have ready the following sauce: put a quart of poivrade sauce in a stewpan, when it boils add twenty French olives (stoned), twenty small pickled onions, and twenty pickled mushrooms; pour the sauce round the beef but not over the potatoes; an ounce of anchovy butter may be added to the sauce if approved of. You can also braise the fillet in a baking dish in the oven with the marinade it is pickled in.

Fillet of Beef à la Romaine.

Trim your fillet and lard it through the thick part with large pieces of cooked tongue and fat bacon, twelve pieces of each, tie it up with a piece of string, put half a pound of butter in a large stewpan, and lay in the beef with a pound of bacon cut in slices, two onions, two bayleaves, two cloves, and ten peppercorns; place it on a sharp fire, when getting a little brown and forming a glaze, put in six glasses of sherry and a pint of consommé, set it over a very slow fire for two hours, moving it round with a wooden spoon occasionally; have ready blanched one pound of the best small maccaroni put it in a stewpan, after it is well drained from the water take up the beef, skim the fat off the gravy it is cooked with, and pass it through a sieve upon the maccaroni, add six tablespoonfuls of tomata sauce, and place it over the fire; when it simmers add half a pound of grated

Parmesan and half a pound of grated Gruyer cheese, move it round quickly, (it must not be too liquid, so if too much gravy from the beef reserve some of it;) season with a little cayenne pepper, salt, and sugar, put a layer of maccaroni upon your dish, then a layer of grated cheese, then the remainder of the maccaroni, egg and bread-crumb the top, sprinkle more grated cheese over, brown it with the salamander, lay the fillet on the top, glaze, and serve very hot. Should any gravy remain pour it round.

Stewed rump of Beef à la Flamande.

Choose a rump of beef from twenty-five to thirty pounds, in weight, the meat dark and well covered with fat, bone and lard it slantwise through and through with very large lardons of fat bacon six inches long, chop up the bone, which put into a large stewpan, with five or six pounds of the trimmings of any other meat, one pound of lean ham, three onions, two turnips, one carrot, one head of celery, one leek, a bunch of parsley, thyme, and bay-leaves, eight peppercorns, and a blade of mace: put a pint of water in the stewpan, cover and stand it over a brisk fire, stirring it occasionally till the bottom is covered with glaze, then lay in the beef, fill the stewpan with water, skim when boiling, and let it simmer on the corner of the fire for six hours; to try when it is done run a trussing-needle into it, if it goes in easy it is done; have ready prepared eighteen middling-sized onions, butter a sauté-pan, put half an ounce of powdered sugar in it, cut a piece of the top and bottom of each onion, blanch them in boiling water ten minutes, drain well, stand them in the sauté-pan, cover with stock, place them over the fire, stew till tender and the stock has become a thin glaze, have ready eighteen pieces of carrots, and eighteen turnips cut in the form of small pears, which dress in the same way as the onions, lay the rump of beef on your dish, and arrange the onions and vegetables with taste around it, using for variety any green vegetables that may happen to be in season with them; for the sauce put a quart of brown sauce in a stewpan, with the glaze from the onions and vegetables, and half a pint of good stock; season with a little pepper and salt if required, reduce a quarter of an hour, or till it becomes rather thick, pour the sauce over the vegetables, glaze the top of the beef, brown it lightly in the oven, or with the salamander, and serve. To carve, cut it in thin slices slantingly through the thickest end, where there is most fat; if underdone it is uneatable.

Stewed Rump of Beef aux Oignons glacés.

Stew the beef as directed in the last, likewise thirty-six onions, stewed in the same way as there directed; make a border of mashed potatoes round the dish, place the beef in the centre, and dress the onions round upon the potato; place a fine Brussels sprout on the top of each onion (or a little sprue grass or green peas if in season), then put a quart of brown sauce in a stewpan, with four spoonfuls of tomata sauce and the glaze the onions were cooked in; boil well five minutes, keeping it stirred and well skimmed, pour over the onions, glaze the beef, brown it with the salamander, and serve. You may put a very white cauliflower at each end of the dish, if you have any. In making the border of mashed potatoes on your dish, be sure and leave sufficient room for the beef, as you can (and it is the best way) dress the onions and garniture on it first, and not place the beef on till ready to serve; for the fat running from the beef it would spoil the appearance of the sauce if it remained long on the dish before serving.

Stewed Rump of Beef à la Voltaire.

Dress the beef as before, then blanch two white winter cabbages (savoys) in salt and water ten minutes; take them out, and lay them on a sieve to drain; then make a mierpoix of two onions, half a carrot, one turnip, one head of celery, one leek, a little parsley, thyme, one bay-leaf, and half a pound of lean ham, all cut up very small; put them into a stewpan with two ounces of butter, fry five minutes, keeping them stirred; then squeeze the cabbage quite dry, lay it in the stewpan with the vegetables and a quart of veal stock, place it over a slow fire to stew for one hour, or till quite tender, take out the cabbage (save the stock), lay it on a cloth, turn the end of the cloth over it, squeeze it rather dry, and make a long roll of it (about the size round of half-a-crown piece), cut it in pieces about an inch in length, and dress them on the dish round the beef; a small onion dressed as before may be placed on the top of each piece with a nice Brussels sprout between; and surround the whole with small fried sausages; for sauce, skim off the fat from the broth the cabbage was stewed in; put half a pint of it in a stewpan, with a quart of brown sauce place it on the fire, and reduce it to one-half; add a quarter of a teaspoonful of sugar, and pour the sauce over the cabbage, glaze and salamander the beef, and serve; this remove is very good, and a similar dish is reputed to have been a great favourite of the celebrated man from whom I have named it.

Stewed Rump of Beef à la Portugaise.

Stew the beef as before, peel eight Portugal onions, boil them in a gallon of water till nearly tender, take them out and drain them; butter a convenient sized stewpan, put in the onions with two ounces of sugar, just cover them with good veal stock, and stew them until the stock is reduced to a thinnish glaze, and adheres to them; place the beef on the dish, and dress the onions round it at equal distances apart, and between each onion place a small but nice white cauliflower; for the sauce, add a quart of brown sauce, with the glaze from the onions; reduce it to half over the fire, pass it through a tammie into a clean stewpan, let it boil, throw in forty French olives ready stoned, pour the sauce over the vegetable, glaze the beef, salamander, and serve.

Stewed Rump of Beef à la Joan d'Arc.

Stew the beef as before, and proceed the same as for Fillet of beef à la Joan d'Arc

Stewed Rump of Beef à la Beyrout.

Stew the beef as before, and proceed as for Filet de bœuf à la Beyrout

Stewed Rump of Beef à la Macédoine de légumes.

Stew the rump as before, then peel forty young carrots, the same number of young turnips; tie up ten small bunches of green spring onions, butter a sauté-pan, place them in it with a tablespoonful of sugar (leave the stalks of the onions about an inch and a half in length), half cover them with some good stock, and let them simmer until quite tender; cook the turnips and carrots in the same manner, but separate, make a low border of mashed potatoes round the dish, leaving room for the beef in the centre; dress the carrots, onions, and turnips on the potatoes tastefully, and variegate them with peas, cauliflowers, asparagus, French beans, and stewed cucumbers glaze and salamander the beef on a separate dish, place it in the middle of the vegetables, and have ready the following sauce: put a quart of brown sauce in a stewpan, with the stocks the vegetables were cooked in, reduce until it becomes thickish, pour over the vegetables, and serve.

Stewed Rump of Beef sauce piquante.

Prepare and stew the rump of beef as before, and prepare the following sauce: put two tablespoonfuls of chopped onions in a stewpan, with six do.

of common vinegar, and half an ounce of glaze; let it reduce to half, then add a quart of brown sauce and half a pint of consommée let it simmer half an hour, skim, and season with a little cayenne pepper, salt, sugar, a tablespoonful of chopped mushrooms, one do. of chopped gherkins, and one do. of sliced gherkins; glaze and salamander the beef, pour the sauce round, and serve.

Stewed Rump of Beef sauce tomate.

Prepare and stew the beef as before, glaze and salamander, pour some tomata sauce round, and serve. If you should have part of a rump of beef left from a previous dinner you can cut it in slices a quarter of an inch thick, and warm them in a little consommée in a sauté-pan; serve with any of the foregoing sauces, but especially the two last; the best way to warm them is to glaze them well and put them in a moderate oven about twenty minutes; do not let them boil, or they would eat very hard.

Stewed Sirloin of Beef.

The sirloin, after having been deprived of its fillet, is of no use for roasting, but is equally as good as the rump when stewed; bone it carefully and lard the thick part with fat bacon, like the rump; roll it up, and tie it well with string, to keep its shape; stew it in the same manner as the rump, trim it at each end, wipe off the greasy fat lightly from the top with a clean cloth, glaze it lightly, and put it in the oven until it has obtained a light gold colour; serve with any of the sauces or garnitures used for stewed rumps of beef.

Stewed Sirloin of Beef à la Printanière.

Prepare and stew a sirloin as described, glaze and salamander it, place a low border of mashed potatoes round the dish, and at each end put a croustade of bread cut in the shape of flat vases; then have ready boiled and cut three inches in length, fifty fine heads of asparagus; dish them in, crown upon the potatoes; then have a quart of very young peas, nicely boiled; put them into a stewpan with a teaspoonful of sugar, a little pepper and salt, and four pats of butter; toss them over the fire till the butter is melted; put them in the croustade at each end of the dish, place the beef in the centre, pour a sauce aux concombres round the beef and serve.

Ribs of Beef à la Jean Bart.

Take four ribs of beef, and saw the rib bones asunder in the middle; pass your knife under, and detach them from the flap; then take the chine bones from the fleshy part, sawing them off the ribs so as to leave but about four inches of the flat rib bones underneath; then lard the thick part through and through with fat bacon like the sirloin, fold the flap over so as to form a nice square piece, tie it with string to keep its shape, and roast three hours in vegetables, in the same manner as described for fillet of beef; when done, take off the string, glaze and salamander, place it on your dish, with a square croustade of bread, with a cannon and anchor also cut from bread upon it, at the head of the dish, and have ready the following sauce: chop very fine ten eschalots, ten fresh mushrooms, and half a pound of lean ham, put them into a stewpan with four glasses of sherry and two of Chili vinegar, add a bunch of parsley, two bay-leaves, the rind of half a lemon, and four cloves; put them into the stewpan, let all simmer ten minutes, then add fifteen spoonfuls of tomata sauce twenty of white sauce and ten do. of consommée; reduce the sauce until rather thick, but it must be transparent, season with a little cayenne pepper, a teaspoonful of sugar, and a little salt, if required; pass it through a tammie into another stewpan, boil it up, and pour round the beef.

Ox Tongues.

May be served plain boiled; if a good-sized tongue, allow it from three to four hours to boil; put it in cold water, take off the skin, trim off a great part of the root, put it in hot water again a short time, dress it on a dish garnished with vegetables as for stewed rump of beef à la Flamande or served with spinach or a Milanaise sauce (see Fillet of Beef à la Milanaise); but when used as a remove, they are mostly served as part of the garniture of another dish.

Loin of Veal à la Cambacères.

Procure a nice white loin of veal, saw off the chump, cut off the thick skin from the thick part, then cut some lardon of fat bacon and lean raw ham, a quarter of an inch square and three inches long, with which lard the thickest end on the top; skewer the flap underneath, butter the bottom of a large flat stewpan, cover with thin slices of fat bacon, and lay the veal on the top of them, the larded side uppermost; add two onions with four cloves stuck in them, one carrot, one turnip, a bunch of parsley, thyme and bay-leaves (tied together), half a pint of bucellas wine, and a quart of stock; place it over a sharp fire a quarter of an hour to boil, skim and place it in a moderate oven for two hours (according to the size), basting it every quarter of an hour with the stock; when done glaze and salamander the larded part, but put the cover of the stewpan over the other part (whilst salamandering it) as it must be kept quite white; make a low border of mashed potatoes on the dish you intend serving it on, and have ready the following garniture: you have previously boiled a Russian ox-tongue; take off the skins, and cut it in escalopes the size of five-shilling pieces; then cut up six very large French truffles, and stew two cucumbers; cut in escalopes of the same size as the tongue, make them hot in separate stewpans, in a little stock, and dress them alternately on the border of mashed potatoes all round the dish; place the veal in the centre, and have ready the following sauce: put two tablespoonfuls of chopped mushrooms in a stewpan with a glass of Madeira wine, two quarts of white sauce   and a pint of boiling milk; reduce it over the fire till it becomes rather thick; pass it through a tammie into another stewpan, season with a little sugar, salt, and the juice of half a lemon; pour a little over each piece of truffle and cucumber, and the rest in the dish; glaze the pieces of tongue carefully, and serve.

Loin of Veal à la Macédoine de légumes.

Prepare and braise the veal as before, garnish and sauce as for stewed rump of beef à la Macédoine de légumes

Loin of Veal à la Purée de Céleri.

Prepare and braise the veal as before, without larding it; make a border of mashed potatoes on the dish, then have twenty good heads of celery, cut off the tops within two inches of the bottom, make a purée of celery   with the tops, and stew the bottoms in a quart of white stock, with a quarter of an ounce of sugar, until tender; dress them upright upon the border of potatoes, place the veal in the centre, and pour the purée of celery round; serve very hot; the sauce must be rather thinner than usual.

Loin of Veal à la Strasbourgienne.

Roast a loin of veal in vegetables in the manner as described for Fillets of Beef   allowing it longer time according to the size; dress it on the dish with a border of mashed potatoes round, then have ready thirty pieces of Strasburg bacon, cut in the shape and size of cutlets; dress them on the potatoes round the veal, pour a sauce poivrade   into the dish, but not over the bacon; glaze the bacon, and serve. The Strasburg bacon being very dry, requires soaking at least twenty-four hours; it most be allowed to simmer until very tender; place it between two dishes, with a weight upon it, and when cold cut it into the shapes required, and make them hot in good white stock. Good streaky bacon may be used instead of the Strasburg, if it is difficult to obtain.

Fillet of Veal à la Princière.

Procure a good leg of veal, cut off the knuckle just above the joint, then cut out the bone from the middle of the fillet; have ready two pounds of forcemeat   cut half a pound of cooked ham and twenty mushrooms into very small dice, mix them with the forcemeat; season rather high with cayenne pepper, salt, and nutmeg, put the forcemeat in the place the bone was taken from, pull the udder of the fillet round, and skewer it up, but not too tight; tie it up with string, put it on a spit, and roast it four hours in vegetables, in the same manner as described for fillets of beef; when done take it from the paper and vegetables, cut off the string, and run three or four silver skewers through it in the place of those you have taken out; the fillet must be quite white; place it on the dish, make a border of mashed potatoes round it, upon which dress alternately a piece of tongue and a piece of bacon, each piece cut in the form of a heart, and not more than a quarter of an inch in thickness; glaze the garniture, and have ready the following sauce: put two quarts of white sauce into a stewpan, stir it over the fire until it becomes thick, then add nearly a pint of thin cream; poor the sauce in the dish, but not over the garniture, and serve immediately; the first slice must be cut off the veal previous to its going to table.

Fillet of Veal à la Versaillienne.

Cut your fillet as before, have ready boiled an ox-tongue, trim it, cut off the root and about two inches of the tip, put it in the middle of the fillet from where you have taken the bone, and fill up the cavities round the tongue with some forcemeat   skewer up the fillet and roast it as before; when done lay it on the dish with a border of mashed potatoes round it, upon which dress alternately a quenelle of veal and a slice of stewed cucumber then put two quarts of white sauce in a stewpan, with a pint of broth, reduce it, and add nearly half a pint of cream, pour the sauce over the garniture, and sprinkle a little chopped tarragon and chervil over it; serve as soon as possible after you have poured the sauce over, which requires to be seasoned rather high.

Fillet of Veal à la Palestine.

Prepare and dress the fillet exactly as before, then peel fifty Jerusalem artichokes, and turn them in the shape of small pears; boil them nicely in salt and water, lay your fillet on a dish with a border of mashed potatoes round it, upon which dress the artichokes, the round part uppermost, between each artichoke place a fine Brussels sprout; sauce the same as the last and serve.

Fillet of Veal à la Jardinière.

Prepare the fillet as before, but place a piece of boiled bacon in the centre instead of the tongue, roast it in vegetables as before, pour a sauce jardinière upon a dish, sprinkle a pint of young green peas plain boiled upon it, dress a cauliflower at each end and another on each side, place the fillet in the middle upon the sauce and serve.

Fillet of Veal à la Potagère.

Prepare the fillet as before, then lard it through and through with pieces of fat bacon a quarter of an inch square and six inches long, skewer it up tight, put it on a spit and roast it as before, but twenty minutes before it is done take it out of the vegetables but not off the spit, and let it remain before the fire to brown; have ready prepared twenty middle-sized onions, and as many pieces of carrots turned in the form of pears, stew them as directed in stewed rump of beef à la Flamande place the fillet in the dish, make a border of mashed potatoes round it, upon which dress the onions and carrots, with a cauliflower at each end; have ready the following sauce: put two quarts of brown sauce in a stewpan, with half a pint of consommé and half the stock the carrots and onions were cooked in, boil it till it becomes like a thin glaze, pour over the vegetables, sprinkle about a pint of young peas nicely boiled over them if in season, and serve.

Fillet of Veal aux petits pois.

Prepare and roast the fillet exactly as the preceding, then put a pint of white sauce in a stewpan, let it boil; have ready a quart of young peas nicely boiled, put them into the stewpan, with the white sauce, a little salt, and half an ounce of pounded sugar, let it boil up, then add two ounces of fresh butter, toss them together over the fire, pour them out into the dish, lay the fillet over, and serve as soon as possible.

Neck of Veal à la purée de céleri.

Take the best end of a neck of veal with about seven bones in it, cut off the chine bones to give it a nice square appearance, and roast it in vegetables as the fillets, but of course it will not require so long; when done, dress it on a dish with a piece of boiled bacon about three inches broad at each end, make a border of mashed potatoes round, upon which dress the bottoms of fifteen heads of stewed celery and sauce with a purée of celery made from the tops, as there directed; serve very hot, but glaze the veal and bacon the last thing before going to table.

Neck of Veal à la Rouennaise.

Prepare a neck of veal, leaving it as long as possible, take off the skin and the chine bones, lard and braise it as for loin of veal à la Cambacères (No. 441); when done, put three tablespoonfuls of oil into a stewpan, with two of chopped eschalots, two of chopped raw mushrooms, and two of chopped parsley, pass them ten minutes over the fire, then pour off the greater part of the oil, add half a teaspoonful of flour, mix it well, and put in eighteen tablespoonfuls of white sauce (No. 7), stir it over the fire till it becomes rather thick, then add a little salt, half a teaspoonful of sugar, and the yolks of two eggs, mix all well together, and spread it over the larded part of the veal, egg and bread-crumb it, brown it lightly with the salamander, and serve a jus d'échalotte sauce (No. 16) with mushrooms in it, pour it in the dish round the veal.

Neck of Veal à la Bruxellaise.

Dress the veal the same as for neck of veal à la purée de céleri then have about one hundred Brussels sprouts, nicely boiled, put them into a stewpan, with two ounces of butter, a little pepper, salt, sugar, and the juice of half a good lemon, stir them gently over the fire but do not break the sprouts, pour them upon your dish, dress the veal upon them with a piece of bacon at each end, glaze them, pour half a pint of thin white sauce (No. 7) round over the Brussels sprouts and serve.

Breast of Veal.

sider that a breast of veal is good without the tendron (which is usually cut out and braised for entrées), yet it would be impossible to roast it with the breast, for it would not be a quarter done by the time the other was; I therefore recommend the following new method: cut out the tendron, braise it as described   let it get cold, take the other bones out of the breast, lay some forcemeat of veal   down the centre, upon which place the tendron, roll it up, sew it with string and your trussing-needle, oil some paper, tie the veal up in it, and roast it two hours, place a sauce Soubise or jardinière on the dish; take the veal from the paper and lay it upon the sauce, or if preferred you may serve with a plain veal sauce made thus: put ten spoonfuls of brown sauce, and the same quantity of melted butter into a stewpan, place it on the fire, let it boil ten minutes, skim it, add three tablespoonfuls of Harvey sauce, and it is ready to serve.

Breast of Veal aux pois fins à l'Anglaise.

Dress the veal exactly as before, have ready boiled a quart of fresh young peas, put them into a stewpan, with eight spoonfuls of brown sauce a teaspoonful of powdered sugar, a quarter of a pound of fresh butter, and a small bunch of parsley, boil them ten minutes, season with a little salt if required, pour them into your dish, glaze the veal and serve it upon them.

Breast of Veal sauce tomate.

Dress the veal as before and serve with a sauce tomate
Breasts of veal may be stewed like the necks, or roasted with vegetables, but they are best roasted as before described.

Calf's Head.

Procure a nice white calf's head that has been well scalded, saw it in halves, taking out the tongue (whole) and the brains, make a white stock as follows: put two carrots, two turnips, two heads of celery, (cut up small), a quarter of a pound of butter, six cloves, four blades of mace, and a bunch of parsley, thyme, and bay-leaves, pass it over the fire twenty minutes in a long brasier large enough to lay the head in, then add a pint of water with which when boiled mix a quarter of a pound of flour, add a gallon of water, two lemons in slices, and a quarter of a pound of salt; let it boil up, then lay the head in, take care that it is well covered or the part exposed would become quite black, when boiling set it on the corner of the stove to simmer for two hours, or until it is done, which you can ascertain by pressing the cheek on the thickest part with your finger, if it gives easily it is done; let it remain in the broth until ready to serve, take it up, drain it on a clean cloth, break off the jaw-bone, lay it on your dish, surround it with six nice boiled potatoes cut in halves, and pour sauce

To serve calf's head for a remove for a large dinner, when the head is done cut off the ears, take out all the bone, and set it on a large dish, place another dish upon it and press it lightly with a seven pounds weight till it gets cold, then lay it out on the table and cut it into oval pieces two inches wide and three long, make a border of mashed potatoes, warm the pieces in the stock it was boiled in, drain them on a cloth, then dish them alternately with quarters of boiled potatoes round the dish, trim the gristly part of the ears, then cut incisions in them longways without separating the edges, turn them over and they will form a frill, place a little of the brains inside of each, and the remainder with the tongue cut in halves in the centre, upon which place the ears at each end, sauce with Hollandaise as before, but if required with other sauce the quarters of potatoes must be omitted.

Calf's Head au naturel.

Although calf's head is seldom if ever dressed this way in England it is about the best method; the glutinous substance of the head being so relishing with this sauce, all French epicures patronise it. Take a small calf's head, lay it upon its skull on the table, open the under part without cutting the tongue, take out the under jaw-bones carefully, fold the cheeks under, tie it round with string, boil it three hours, (as described in the last), when done lay it upon a cloth to drain, untie the string, take out the tongue, peel it, put the point of a knife in the middle of the skull bone, it will open with facility, take off the two pieces of bone that cover the brains, and leave them exposed, place the head upon a dish with one half of the tongue on each side, (each person that partakes of it should be served with tongue and brains); serve the following sauce in a boat: put two tablespoonfuls of chopped eschalots, one of chopped parsley, one of chopped tarragon and chervil, a quarter ditto of salt, a little pepper, six tablespoonfuls of salad oil, and three ditto of common vinegar; mix all well together and serve; each person should stir the sauce previous to helping themselves to it, for by standing the oil will come to the top; the head requires to be very hot, but the sauce quite cold.

Half a Calf's Head à la Luxembourg.

Procure half a calf's head, pass your knife under the skin upon the top of the skull and saw off about two inches of the skull bone, boil it as described in the last, when done drain it on a cloth, lay it in a sauté-pan, and spread the following forcemeat over it: having previously well washed the brains, cut them in slices, put two ounces of butter in a sauté-pan, let it melt, then lay in the brains, sprinkle a little chopped parsley, pepper, salt, and the juice of half a lemon; put them over a slow fire, turn them, and when done chop them fine and put them in a basin, with four tablespoonfuls of bread-crumbs, one of chopped mushrooms, a little more pepper and salt, a little grated nutmeg, and chopped lemon peel; mix altogether, with the yolks of two eggs; after it is spread wash it over with eggs, with a paste-brush, sprinkle some bread-crumbs over it, place it in the oven half an hour, salamander a light brown, place it on a dish, and have ready the following sauce: put into a stewpan four tablespoonfuls of tarragon vinegar, one blade of mace, two cloves, one spoonful of scraped horseradish, and a glass of brandy; let it boil five minutes, add three pints of brown sauce   and one ditto of consommé   when it boils set it at the corner of the stove, skim it well and reduce it to two-thirds, pass it through a tammie into a clean stewpan, and add two dozen of pickled mushrooms, and two dozen very small gherkins; warm altogether, finish with an ounce of anchovy butter, and half a teaspoonful of sugar, pour the sauce round the head and serve; you may dress the whole head, cutting it up as described
cover each piece with the forcemeat, dress them on a border of mashed potatoes, and serve the sauce in the centre.

Tête de Veau en Tortue.

Dress the head, and when cold cut it in oval pieces,
       make a small elevated casserole of rice in the shape of an oval vase
          which place in the centre of the dish, make the pieces hot and dish them on a border of mashed potatoes round it, placing an ear at each end; have ready the following garniture and sauce: make a mierepoix of two onions, one turnip, half a carrot, a quarter of a pound of lean ham, all cut up in slices; put them into a stewpan, with two cloves, half a blade of mace, a sprig of thyme, marjoram, winter savory, basil, a little parsley, a bay-leaf, and two ounces of butter; pass it over a fire till it becomes a little brown, then add four glasses of Madeira, two quarts of brown sauce   half a pint of tomata sauce   and half a pint of broth, reduce it on a quick

fire twenty minutes, skim it well, pass it through a tammie into a clean stewpan, boil it again till it adheres to the back of the spoon, season with half a saltspoonful of cayenne pepper, and a little sugar, add twenty prepared cockscombs six French truffles sliced, twenty blanched mushrooms, and twenty small quenelles when very hot lay the garniture in the rice casserole, and pour the sauce over the pieces of calf's head; an attelet with a crawfish, truffle, and large quenelle upon it, may be stuck at each end of the casserole of rice in a slanting direction.

Calf's Head à la Pottinger.

Dress and cut a head in pieces as before, make two croustades of bread, one in the shape of a cushion, and the other like a scallop-shell, make the pieces of head hot, and dress them in your dish on a border of rice (prepared put the croustade in the form of a cushion at one end of the dish, and the other elevated upon a piece of fried bread at the other end, in which put the brains, at each side of the dish dress an ear cut to form a frill, with a plover's egg in each; have ready the following sauce: put two tablespoonfuls of chopped onions into a stewpan, with six of the vinegar from Indian pickles, let it boil a few minutes, then add three pints of white sauce and a pint of white stock, let it boil until it adheres to the back of the spoon, pass it through a tammie into another stewpan, add twenty mild Indian pickles, the same number of small gherkins, and thirty cockscombs when hot pour the sauce over the head, stick three attelets prepared as in the last in the croustade resembling a cushion very tastefully, and serve.

Calf's Head in currie.

Prepare and dish the head as in the last, boil a pound of rice and dish it in a pyramid in the middle, leaving a place at the top to lay in the brains; have ready prepared the following sauce: put four onions, two apples (cut in slices), a sprig of thyme, a little parsley, a blade of mace, and six cloves into a stewpan, with two ounces of butter, fry them of a light brown, add one tablespoonful of curry powder, mix it well, then add three pints of white sauce and a pint of broth; boil altogether twenty minutes, pass it through a tammie, put it again into a stewpan, let it boil, season with a little salt and sugar, pour over the head and serve very hot. If the currie is preferred browner, use a little brown gravy more currie powder may be added if required very hot.

Saddle of Mutton à la Brétonne.

Roast a saddle of mutton quite plain (see kitchen at home), for the sauce wash and soak well a pint of young dry French haricots, put them into a large stewpan with three quarts of water (cold), an ounce of salt, and an ounce of butter; set them over a brisk fire till they boil, then set them at the corner and let them simmer for five hours, or till tender, drain them on a sieve, cut four onions in thin slices, put them in a stewpan, with three ounces of butter, stir them over the fire till they are a light brown colour, then add half a tablespoonful of flour (mix it well), and a pint of good gravy; when it boils put in the haricots, mix them well, and season with a saltspoonful of pepper, and four ditto of salt, add the gravy from the mutton, with half an ounce of glaze, pour them on the dish, dress the saddle on the top and serve. Care must be taken not to have this sauce either too thick or too thin.

Saddle of Mutton au Laver.

Roast the saddle quite plain, put two pounds of fresh laver in a stewpan, with two tablespoonfols of catsup, four ounces of butter, a teaspoonful of salt, a little pepper, four tablespoonfuls of brown sauce, and one ounce of glaze, make it very hot, pour in the dish, dress the saddle upon it and serve.

Saddle of Mutton à la Polonaise.

Roast a middling-sized saddle of mutton, and let it get cold, then cut off all the meat, leaving the bone and flaps uncut, stand it on a strong dish that will bear the oven; have ready some mashed potatoes rather stiff with which build a wall round the bone and flaps, to shape it, again like the saddle, mince the meat you have cut out very fine, put two tablespoonfuls of chopped onions in a middling-sized stewpan, with half an ounce of butter, fry them a very light brown, then add half a tablespoonful of flour (mix well), a quart of brown sauce and half a pint of stock, let it boil ten minutes, then add the mutton (mix well), season with pepper, salt, and two tablespoonfuls of catsup, make it quite hot, then add three yolks of eggs, stir well over the fire for three minutes to set the eggs, put it into the saddle, egg all over with a paste-brush, cover the top with bread-crumbs, melt a little butter, which sprinkle over the bread-crumbs, put it in a moderate oven half an hour, salamander a light brown, serve in the same dish, and pour the following sauce round; put a pint of brown sauce in a stewpan, with half a pint of broth, a spoonful of catsup, half a teaspoonful of sugar, and the smallest piece of garlick imaginable scraped on the tip of a knife, boil altogether five minutes, it is then ready. This dish may be made of the remains of a saddle of mutton left from a previous dinner, by procuring sufficient mutton for mincing, and is equally as good.

Saddle of Mutton à la Marseillaise.

Prepare the saddle of mutton exactly as for Polonaise, only when you put in the mince, which you have made rather stiffer, have ready prepared the following purée: cut six onions in small dice, put them into a stewpan with two ounces of butter, let them simmer gently until quite tender, then add half a tablespoonful of flour (mix well), four ditto of white sauce (No. 7), and ten of milk, let it boil twenty minutes, season with a little pepper, salt, and sugar, stir in the yolks of three eggs, stir over the fire a minute to set the eggs, let it cool a little, and spread it over the mince, egg over and breadcrumb the top, put it in a moderate oven half an hour, salamander a light brown, and serve with a sauce Soubise rather thinnish round it.

Saddle of Mutton rôti, braisé, à la Mirabeau.

Trim a nice saddle of mutton (South Down are the best, from four to five years old), take off the skin and skewer the flaps underneath, roast it in vegetables as directed for fillet of beef about two hours and a half will be sufficient, take it from the vegetables, glaze and salamander nicely, place it on your dish and serve with the following sauce: put a quart of poivrade sauce in a stewpan, and when boiling add a teaspoonful of sugar, four of chopped gherkins, and two ounces of boiled beetroot cut in dice; sauce over and serve.

Saddle of Mutton, rôti, braisé, aux légumes glacé.

Roast the saddle in vegetables as in the last, glaze and salamander, dress on your dish with a border of mashed potatoes round, upon which dress your vegetables prepared as for stewed rump of beef à la Flamande pouring the same sauce over them.

Haunch of Mutton.

This delicate joint is generally plain roasted (see Kitchen at Home); when of the first quality and properly kept it is by many compared to venison, although there is not the least resemblance, the fat of venison being so very delicate and palatable that nothing can equal it, but both are very estimable. I shall give but a few simple receipts in order to preserve the flavour of this delicate joint.

Haunch of Mutton au jus de Groseilles.

Roast the haunch quite plain, put twenty tablespoonfuls of brown sauce in a stewpan, with ten of consommé one of tomata sauce and an ounce of glaze, boil it gently half an hour, then add four tablespoonfuls of red currant jelly, boil up, pour it on the dish, and the moment you serve lay the haunch upon it; should you dish the haunch too soon the fat would run from it and spoil the sauce; it should be carved in the same way as a haunch of venison, then you keep the gravy from running into the sauce, and can serve it separately.

Haunch of Mutton à la Polonaise.

Roast a haunch, and when cold cut out all the meat from the middle, leaving the edges (or the mashed potatoes would not stand), mince the meat, shape the haunch with mashed potatoes, and proceed as for the saddle You can use a haunch left from a previous dinner, if not too much cut.

Haunch of Mutton à la Bohémienne.

Procure a small haunch of mutton of about twelve pounds in weight, beat it well with a rolling-pin, lay it in an earthen pan, and cover with a marinade as prepared for fillet of beef let it remain a week, roast it in paste in the same manner as for the haunch of venison roast it three hours, take it out of the paste, glaze and salamander of a nice brown colour, put a frill of paper to the knuckle, and dress upon your dish with the following sauce round it: pass half a pint of the marinade it was pickled in through a sieve into a stewpan, add a quart of brown sauce let it boil till it becomes rather thick, skim well, add one tablespoonful of red currant jelly, pass through a tammie into a clean stewpan, then add twenty blanched mushrooms, twenty small pickled onions, and twenty French olives (stoned); let them warm in the sauce, which slightly flavour with a little scraped garlick sauce over.

Leg of Mutton à la Provençale.

Procure a nice delicate leg of mutton, beat it well with a rolling-pin, make an incision at the knuckle in which push four cloves of garlick as deep into the fleshy part of the leg as you can, roast it quite plain, and serve a thin sauce à la Brétonne under it, into which you have put a small piece of scraped garlick.

Gigot de Mouton de sept heures.

What! seven hours to cook a leg of mutton! exclaims John Bull; shade of the third George protect us, why 'tis nonsense; to which I must answer you are right, it would rob it of its flavour; but still it gains another flavour which is far from being bad; and you must observe that, although there will be less nourishment it will be much easier of digestion. Well, well, methinks I hear him say, if you are determined upon publishing that destructive receipt (which absurdity I am sure no one upon this soil will ever follow, or disgrace their tables with), write it in French and offend no one; but for heaven's sake never invite me to dine with you on the day you find room for such a dish upon your table, so taking the hint I give it in my native tongue:—Désosse un assez gros gigot de mouton jusqu'à la moitié du manche; vous assaisonnerez des lardons de sel, de gros poivre, de thyme et de laurier pilés, et vous piquerez le dedans de votre gigot; ne faites pas sortir vos lardons par-dessous. Quand il est bien piqué, vous lui ferez prendre sa forme première; vous le ficellerez de manière qu'on ne s'aperçoive pas qu'on l'ait désossé; vous mettrez ensuite des bardes de lard au fond de votre braisière, quelques tranches de jambon, les os concassés, quelques tranches de mouton, quatre carottes, six oignons, trois feuilles de laurier, un peu de thyme, trois clous de girofle, un bouquet de persil et de ciboule, deux cuillerées à pot de bouillon: vous mettrez à cuire votre gigot pendant sept heures, et le ferez aller à très petit feu; vous en mettrez aussi sur le couvercle de la braisière. Au moment de servir vous l'égoutterez, vous le déficellerez, le glacerez, et le servirez avec le mouillement réduit dans lequel il aura cuit; ayant soin de bien-écumer toute la graisse que votre fond est susceptible d'avoir.

Necks of Mutton à la Légumière.

Cut off the scrags and take the chine bones from two necks of mutton, lard the lean parts with lardons of fat bacon about three inches long, roast them in vegetables as for fillet of beef ; when done, dress them on a dish, placing fillet to fillet, so as to form a saddle; fill up the crevice between them with mashed potatoes, upon which dress small pieces of cauliflower and small bunches of asparagus, or Brussels sprouts; make a border of mashed potatoes round the mutton, upon which dress some onions, with pieces of carrots and turnips stewed (see stewed rump of beef à la Flamande, place four onions at each end of the dish, and stick a fine head of asparagus in each; glaze the mutton, and pour a demi-glace over the vegetables.

Necks of Mutton à la Bretonne.

Trim the necks as above, roast them quite plain (see Kitchen at Home), and sauce as for saddle of mutton à la Bretonne,

Neck of Mutton à la Bohémienne.

Proceed as for haunch of mutton only three days in the marinade will be sufficient.

Neck of Mutton à la Provençale.

Trim a neck of mutton, lard it, and put it into a convenient sized stewpan, with two onions, one carrot, one turnip (cut in slices), six cloves, a blade of mace, and a bunch of parsley, thyme and bay-leaves; cover with white broth, and set it on the fire; when boiling, set it on the corner to simmer for two hours; take it out, and lay it on a sauté-pan, spread a purée of onions as for cotelettes de mouton à la Provençale over the top, egg and bread-crumb it, put it in the oven a quarter of an hour, salamander a light brown, sauce with demi-glace as for the cotelettes.

Neck of Mutton à la Charte.

Trim two necks of mutton as before, lard and braise as in the last article; then peel some young turnips, and cut about a pint of scoops from them the size of marbles (with an iron scoop); put a teaspoonful of powdered sugar into a stewpan, place it over a sharp fire, and just as it begins to brown, add two ounces of butter, and the scooped turnips; pass them ten minutes over the fire, then add a pint and a half of brown sauce and half a pint of consommée; let it simmer till the turnips are quite done; take them out, and put them into another stewpan, skim and reduce the sauce until it becomes rather thickish, season a little more if required and pass it through a tammie upon the turnips, dress the necks upon a dish fillet to fillet to form a saddle; glaze, pour the sauce and turnips round, have twelve pieces of turnips cut in the form of pears and stewed as dress six of them, one upon the other, in pyramids at each end of the dish, and serve very hot.

Breast of Mutton panée, grillée, sauce piquante.

Procure two breasts of mutton cut as large as possible, which put in a stewpan, and braise three hours in the same manner as described for neck of mutton Provençale previous to placing them in the stewpan tie them well up with string; when done take up, lay them on a dish, take all the string and bones from them, which will leave with facility, place another dish upon them, and press till quite cold with a fourteen pounds weight; about half an hour before serving trim, egg and bread-crumb, beat gently with a knife, melt a little butter in a stewpan, and with a paste-brush butter the mutton all over, throw them again into bread-crumbs, beat gently again with your knife, and put them on the gridiron over a moderate fire; when lightly browned on one side, turn them by placing another gridiron over and turning both gridirons together; when done, take them from the gridiron with a fish-slice, lay on your dish, and serve sauce piquante round, or you may serve them with dressed spinach sauce Soubise or fines herbes

Saddle of Lamb aux petits pois.

Roast a saddle of lamb in vegetables, as described for fillet of beef when done glaze and salamander a light brown colour; put a quart of young peas boiled very green into a stewpan, quite hot, with two ounces of butter, half a tablespoonful of sugar, a little salt, and six tablespoonfuls of bechamel sauce shake them round over the fire a few minutes, pour them in your dish, and dress the saddle over. A saddle will require about two hours roasting.

Saddle of Lamb à la Sévigné.

Roast the saddle with vegetables as before, make a purée d'asperges cut two large cucumbers in pieces about two inches and a half in length; cut each piece lengthwise in three, take out the cores, cut them in the shape of the bowl of a spoon, and stew them as described have ready some quenelles de volaille place a roll of mashed potatoes at each end of the dish; at the bottom dress half a circle, with the cucumber and quenelles, by laying them alternately in a slanting position, and at the top of the dish lay nine quenelles upon a roll of potatoes, formed like the bows of a boat, so that the first quenelle stands out in a point, and the others are brought gradually in to the ends; place a piece of stewed cucumber cut like a diamond between each quenelle, and dress some nice heads of sprue grass in the centre, at each end of the dish; place the saddle in the middle, and pour the purée d'asperges (quite hot) on each side.

Saddle of Lamb à l'Indienne.

Roast the saddle in vegetables as before, then put a quart of sauce à l'Indienne into a stewpan; when boiling and ready to serve, add thirty very mild green Indian pickles. When hot, sauce round and serve.

Saddle of Lamb demi Provençale.

Roast the saddle with vegetables as before; cut six large onions in small dice, which put into a stewpan with three tablespoonfuls of oil; stir over a slow fire till they are quite tender, then add half a tablespoonful of flour (mix well) and twelve do. of white sauce boil ten minutes, season with half a teaspoonful of salt, one do. of sugar, and a quarter do. of pepper;

add the yolks of three eggs, stir it over the fire half a minute, lay it out on a dish, and when nearly cold spread it over the saddle a quarter of an inch in thickness; egg and bread-crumb over, put it in a sharp oven ten minutes, salamander of a light brown, and serve with sauce demi-glace round it.

Saddle of Lamb à la Ménagère.

Plain roast a saddle[6] and allow it to get cold, cut out all the meat, leaving the flaps untouched, shape round the saddle a wall of stiff mashed potatoes, cut the meat up in square thin slices, then put a quart of white sauce in a stewpan; let it boil up, put in your meat, season with lemon-juice, pepper, and salt; moisten with a little white broth, and when it is quite hot add the yolks of two eggs, mixed with four spoonfuls of cream; place it within the saddle, egg all over, sprinkle bread-crumbs on the top, and put it in a sharp oven upon the dish you intend serving it on a quarter of an hour; have ready poached eight eggs, lay them on the top, garnish round with peas, Brussels sprouts, or asparagus, nicely boiled, and pour a white demi-glace round; serve immediately; ham or tongue, with mushrooms cut in slices, may be added with the lamb.

Haunch of Lamb.

Like the haunch of mutton, this joint is usually plain roasted, but for a change it may be roasted with vegetables, and served with any of the sauces, as used for the saddle in the foregoing receipts. It will require nearly two hours roasting.

The fore-quarter may likewise be dressed the same ways.

Fore-quarter of Lamb à l'Hôtelière.

Roast a fore-quarter well covered with oiled paper, and a good distance from the fire, when done it must be a light gold colour, then put a quarter of a pound of maître d'hôtel butter in a stewpan, and when beginning to melt add half a pint of good cream; shake the stewpan round till hot, but not near boiling, and the moment you serve pour it upon the dish, and dress the fore-quarter upon it.

Fore-quarter of House Lamb aux pointes d'asperges.

Roast the lamb exactly as in the last, have ready a sauce aux pointes d'asperges pour it hot on your dish, lay the lamb upon it, and serve. It will take about an hour roasting.

Ribs of Lamb à la Chancelière.

Roast a fore-quarter of lamb with vegetables and when done cut out the shoulder very round, cut off all the meat from it, and mince it very fine, with half a pound of cooked ham, twenty button mushrooms, and six middling-sized French truffles; then put a teaspoonful of chopped eschalot in a stewpan, with a teaspoonful of salad oil; fry them of a light yellow colour, add a quarter of a tablespoonful of flour (mix well), half a pint of stock, and a pint of white sauce; let it boil, keeping it stirred, add your meat and the other ingredients, season with pepper and salt, and when boiling add the yolks of two eggs; stir them in quickly, and pour the whole into the place you cut the shoulder from; egg it over with a paste-brush, sprinkle bread-crumbs and grated Parmesan cheese over, brown it lightly with the salamander, dress upon your dish, pour a sauce bechamel à la crème

Leg of Lamb à la St. John.

Roast the leg in vegetables as described an hour and a half would be sufficient; when done, place a paper frill on the knuckle, and lay it in your dish; have ready prepared the following sauce: put the yolks of three eggs in a stewpan, with half a pound of fresh butter, the juice of half a lemon, a little pepper, salt, and two tablespoonfuls of tarragon vinegar; place it over a moderate fire, keeping it stirred with a wooden spoon, and when the butter has melted and begins to thicken (great care must be taken that the eggs do not curdle, which they will do if you allow it to get too hot before the butter is melted, or allow it to boil in the least), add a pint of white sauce and a little sugar; mix all well together, pass through a tammie into a clean stewpan, place again over the fire to get hot (but not to boil), keeping it stirred; add half a gill of cream, and if too thick a little milk, pour it over the lamb, have ready a few pistachios each cut in eight lengthwise, sprinkle over, and serve very hot.

Leg of Lamb aux pois.

Roast a leg of lamb quite plain, have ready boiled, very green, two quarts of young peas, put them hot into a stewpan, with three pats of butter, a tablespoonful of sugar, a little pepper, salt, and six spoonfuls of white sauce mix all well together over the fire, without breaking the peas; pour them in a dish, dress the leg over and serve.

Boiled Leg of Lamb and Spinach.

Boil a leg of lamb quite plain, which will take from an hour and a quarter to an hour and a half (add a little milk to the water you boil it in), have ready dressed sufficient spinach to cover the bottom of the dish an inch and a half in thickness, dress the lamb upon it, and serve; to dress spinach

Roast Leg of Lamb à la Jardinière.

Plain roast the lamb, have ready a sauce jardinière pour it on the dish, and dress the leg upon it.

The shoulder may be dressed exactly as the leg.

Shoulder of Lamb à la Bruxellaise.

Roast a shoulder of lamb with vegetables, and serve with sauce as for neck of veal à la Bruxellaise

Shoulder of Lamb à la Polonaise.

Cut all the meat from the top of the shoulder and a little from the bottom, so as not to spoil the shape; build a wall of mashed potatoes about two inches high round it, and proceed as for saddle of mutton

PORK.

Pork is a great favourite with some persons but scarcely ever used for removes, except plain roasted stuffed with sage and onions, that I shall describe in my Kitchen at Home, but I shall here give six new ways of dressing pork for removes; it must be of the best quality, small, and, above all, in season.

Leg of Pork sauce Robert.

Score the skin of the leg with a sharp knife, oil some paper, wrap the leg up in it, and roast about two hours and a half of a nice yellow colour; have ready the following sauce: put four tablespoonfuls of chopped onions into a stewpan, with two ounces of butter, stir over a moderate fire till the onions are nicely browned, then add three tablespoonfuls of tarragon vinegar (let it boil), a quart of brown sauce   half a pint of consommé, and a little brown gravy; let it boil at the corner of the stove about twenty minutes, skim it well, reduce it till it adheres to the spoon, season with a little cayenne pepper, salt, and two tablespoonfuls of French mustard; when ready to serve add twenty small gherkins, twenty pickled mushrooms, twenty small quenelles   pour the sauce in the dish, dress the leg upon it, put a paper frill on the knuckle and serve.

Leg of Pork à la Piedmontaise.

Roast the leg as before, and prepare the sauce thus: put two tablespoonfuls of chopped onions into a stewpan, with four of Indian pickle vinegar, let boil a few minutes, then add twenty tablespoonfuls of brown sauce   and ten ditto of consommé, let boil twenty minutes, skim well, season with a little cayenne pepper, sugar, and salt, pass it through a tammie into a clean stewpan, stone forty French olives, put them into the sauce, glaze the pork and pour the sauce round.

Loin of Pork à la Bourguignote.

Trim a small loin of pork, cut off all the rind, wrap it in oiled paper, and roast of a nice yellow colour; have ready the following preparation: cut six large onions in small dice and put them in a stewpan, with two ounces of butter; let them stew over a slow fire till quite tender and rather brown, then add half a tablespoonful of flour (mix well), and fifteen of brown sauce boil twenty minutes, season with a teaspoonful of chopped sage, half ditto of sugar, and half of salt, finish with the yolks of three eggs, stir over the fire half a minute to set the eggs, and spread it over the pork half an inch in thickness, egg and bread-crumb over it, place it in the oven ten minutes, salamander a light brown, and serve the following sauce round it: put fifteen spoonfuls of brown sauce and six of consommé in a stewpan, with two of Harvey sauce, one of catsup, and half a one of Chili vinegar, boil altogether ten minutes, and finish with a little sugar, salt, and pepper, if required.

Neck of Pork à la Remoulade, à l'Indienne.

Trim the neck, but do not take off the rind, wrap it in oiled paper and roast as previously; make a good sauce remoulade to which add three tablespoonfuls of chopped Indian pickle, pour the sauce in the dish and dress the pork upon it.

Neck of Pork à la Vénitienne.

Put two tablespoonfuls of chopped onions into a stewpan, with an ounce of butter, fry rather brown, then add half a tablespoonful of flour (mix well), and twelve ditto of brown sauce, reduce it until thick, add half a tablespoonful of chopped parsley, one ditto of chopped mushrooms, and season with half a teaspoonful of sugar, a little salt, and cayenne pepper; let it cool, open part of the neck lengthwise between the skin and the flesh, put in the above preparation, tie up the neck in oiled paper and roast it, then prepare the following sauce: put two chopped eschalots in a stewpan, with a spoonful of salad oil, two tablespoonfuls of common vinegar, and a small piece of glaze; boil five minutes, then add six tablespoonfuls of brown sauce six of consommé, and six ditto of tomata sauce boil altogether ten minutes, pour the sauce on your dish and serve the pork upon it.

Roast Sucking Pig.

Procure a sucking pig of from eight to nine pounds, wash the inside and wipe it well with a dry cloth, prepare the stuffing thus: boil four large onions until quite tender, chop them very fine, with six leaves of sage, a little thyme and parsley, season with a little cayenne pepper and salt, add three tablespoonfuls of bread-crumbs, and mix it with three eggs, stuff the pig quite full, sew up the belly, put it on the spit, place it at a distance from a moderate fire (folded in buttered paper) for half an hour, then put it closer, allowing it two hours to roast, but ten minutes before it is done take off all the paper to allow it to become brown and crisp; serve plain gravy in the dish, and bread sauce with currants in it in a boat; before sending it to table take off the head and cut the pig in halves down the back.

Sucking Pig à la Savoyarde.

Take a very delicate sucking pig and prepare the following stuffing: put two tablespoonfuls of chopped onions in a stewpan, with a teaspoonful of oil, pass them over a moderate fire five minutes, add half a pound of rice previously well boiled in stock, half a pound of sausage-meat, four pats of butter, a little chopped parsley, pepper, salt, and three eggs; mix all well together, stuff the pig, and roast it in oiled paper, as in the last; prepare the sauce thus: put two tablespoonfuls of chopped onions in a stewpan, with one of salad oil and fry them quite white, add a wineglassful of sherry or Madeira, a pint of white sauce and six tablespoonfuls of milk, let it boil a quarter of an hour, skim well, add a good tablespoonful of chopped mushrooms, half ditto of chopped parsley, a teaspoonful of sugar, ditto of salt, and a little white pepper; dress the pig in the dish, pour the sauce round, and garnish with small fried sausages.

Turkey à la Nelson.

Make a croustade resembling the head of a ship, as represented in the design; procure a very white nice young turkey, truss it as for boiling, leaving as much of the skin of the neck attached to the breast as possible, have ready the following stuffing: scrape an ounce of fat bacon (with a knife), put it into a stewpan, with a teaspoonful of chopped eschalots, pass five minutes over a moderate fire, then add twenty tablespoonfuls of white sauce let it reduce till thick, add twenty small heads of mushrooms, six French truffles cut in slices, and twelve cockscombs; mix all well together over the fire, season with a teaspoonful of powdered sugar, half ditto of salt, and a little white pepper; finish with the yolks of two eggs, stir over the fire a minute to set the eggs, and lay it out on a dish to get cold, then detach the skin on the breast from the flesh without breaking, and force some of the stuffing under the skin; put the remainder in the interior of the breast, roast it in vegetables as described for fillet of beef but just before it is done take away the paper and vegetables, and let it remain before the fire till of a fine gold colour. Fix the croustade at the head of the dish with a paste made of white of egg and flour, make a border of mashed potatoes round the dish, place the turkey in the centre, and have ready the following garniture: fillet three fowls, lard and braise the fillets as form the legs into little ducklings as described prepare six slices of tongue of the size and shape of the fillets, and dress them round the turkey upon the mashed potatoes to form a ship. For the sauce put two glasses of Madeira wine in a stewpan, with a tablespoonful of Chili vinegar, two minced apples, a small bunch of parsley, a spoonful of chopped mushrooms, and half an ounce of glaze; let it boil a few minutes, add ten tablespoonfuls of tomata sauce a quart of brown sauce and a pint of consommé, let it boil quickly until it adheres to the spoon, stirring it the whole time, finish with a tablespoonful of red currant jelly, pass it through a tammie into another stewpan, season with a little salt and pepper, boil it another minute, glaze the turkey, pour the sauce in the dish, glaze the pieces of tongue and serve.

Turkey à la Godard.

Procure a good-sized turkey, very white and well covered with fat, truss it as for boiling, hold the breast over a charcoal fire till the flesh is set, then lard it with fat bacon very neatly, lay the turkey in a braising-pan breast upwards, and pour in as much good veal stock as will nearly reach the larded part, start it to boil, skim, then place it over a slow fire to simmer for three hours, keeping some live charcoal upon the cover of the braising-pan, and now and then moistening the breast with a little of the stock; when done take it up, give a nice yellow colour to the bacon on the breast, put it on your dish, and have ready the following garniture: prepare six large quenelles de volaille truss and roast four pigeons lard and cook four fine veal sweetbreads arrange them with taste round the turkey, and have ready the following sauce: strain half the stock the turkey was dressed in through a cloth into a stewpan, let it boil, put it on the corner of the stove, skim till you get off every particle of grease, reduce it to half, add a quart of brown sauce and half a pint of tomata sauce let boil, keeping it stirred till becoming a thickish demi-glace, add two dozen cockscombs, and a teaspoonful of sugar, with a little cayenne and salt if required, pour it in the dish but not over the garniture, and serve. Attelets of cockscombs and truffles are sometimes stuck in the breast, but it is an impediment to the carving, and it looks as well without.

Turkey à la Chipolata.

Although this dish has been degusted by our great great grandfathers, and has been for upwards of a century one of the strongest pillars of the art, I shall here describe it, as an old proverb justly reminds me that a good thing can never get old. Truss the turkey as for boiling, and to modernize it, lard neatly the right breast, roast thirty good chesnuts which mix in a basin with one pound of sausage-meat highly seasoned, stuff the breast of the turkey with it, and braise as in the last article, when done place it upon your dish, and have ready the following ragout: cut two pounds of lean bacon in long square pieces about the size of walnuts, blanch them ten minutes in boiling water, put two ounces of butter in a middling-sized stewpan, with the bacon, fry till becoming rather yellowish, then add a tablespoonful of flour, mix well, add by degrees three pints of good white stock, with a quart of white sauce, stir over the fire till boiling, then put in forty button onions, twenty fine heads of mushrooms, a bunch of parsley, one bay-leaf, and two cloves; boil altogether, and when the onions are done take them with the mushrooms and bacon out of the sauce with a colander spoon, put them into a clean stewpan, with thirty chestnuts roasted white, and eight sausages broiled, each one cut in three, reduce the sauce, keeping it stirred till it becomes the thickness of brown sauce, previously having simmered, and skimmed off all the grease, pass the sauce through a tammie upon the other ingredients, make all hot together, finish with a liaison of two yolks of eggs, and pour over and round the turkey (except over the breast), which serve very hot. The old style used to be brown, in that case substitute brown sauce for white and omit the liaison.

Small Turkey à la Duchesse.

Procure a small nice turkey, truss it as for boiling, and roast it in vegetables as usual, keeping it quite white, place it upon your dish with a border of mashed potatoes round, upon which dress twenty-five quenelles and twelve slices of tongue (cut in the same shape as the quenelles), have ready boiled very green some French beans cut in diamond shapes, which sprinkle over the breast of the turkey, and sauce over with a purée de concombres

Poularde à l'Ambassadrice.

Procure a nice white poularde, cut it open down the back, and bone it without breaking the skin, make two pounds of forcemeat with which mix six large French truffles cut in slices, spread the forcemeat half an inch in thickness upon the inside of the poularde, then have ready boiled and nicely trimmed a small ox tongue, cover it with the forcemeat, fold a slice of fat bacon round, and put it in the middle of the poularde, which roll up and sew from end to end, fold the poularde in slices of fat bacon, and tie it up in a cloth, have ready prepared some vegetables of all kinds cut in slices, put them in a convenient-sized stewpan, lay the poularde upon them, the breast downwards, but first moisten the vegetables with a little salad oil, add half a pint of Madeira wine, and sufficient white broth to cover the poularde, set on a sharp fire to boil, skim, and let it simmer for three hours, prepare the following garniture: braise two spring chickens (trussed as for boiling) three quarters of an hour in the braise with the poularde, have ready prepared a croustade as represented in the design, upon which place a larded sweetbread nicely cooked and glazed, place a fine cockscomb and a large truffle upon a silver attelet, and run it through the sweetbread, sticking it upright in the croustade, then take the poularde out of the cloth, take off the bacon, pull out the string it was sewed up with, dry it with a cloth, and place it upon your dish with the garniture arranged tastefully around it; have ready the following sauce: chop half a pottle of fresh mushrooms very fine, put them into a stewpan, with one ounce of butter and the juice of half a lemon, boil over a sharp fire five minutes, add two quarts of white sauce with one of the braise, let boil, keeping it stirred, until it adheres to the back of the spoon, rub it through a tammie into a clean stewpan, adding a few spoonfuls of white broth if too thick, season with a teaspoonful of sugar and a little salt, cut a few very black truffles in slices, and chop a couple very fine, place them on a plate in the hot closet ten minutes; put your sauce again on the fire, and when boiling add a gill of whipped cream, pour the sauce over the poularde and chickens, lay the slices of truffles here and there upon them, and sprinkle the chopped truffles lightly over, the blackness of the truffles contrasting with the whiteness of the sauce has a pleasing effect; serve directly you have poured the sauce and sprinkled the truffles over. The bones being taken out of the poularde they must be carved crosswise, thus carving through tongue and all.

Poulardes en Diadème.

Make a croustade representing a diadem, stick three silver attelets upon it, on which you have stuck a crawfish, a large truffle, and a large quenelle, roast two poulardes quite white in vegetables, and have an ox tongue nicely boiled and trimmed, place them on the dish with their tails to the croustade and the tongue between; upon the root of the tongue and at the end of each poularde place a nice larded sweetbread well cooked and glazed (or a fine head of cauliflower nicely boiled), make a border of mashed potatoes round, upon which dress alternately truffles and fine cockscombs, previously dressed   have ready the following sauce: peel four middling-sized cucumbers, mince and put them into a stewpan with an ounce of butter, a quarter of a pound of lean ham, two chopped eschalots, and a little powdered sugar, pass the whole over a slow fire, and stew them gently half an hour, or till quite tender, then mix in half an ounce of flour, add two quarts of white sauce   which moisten with a pint of white broth, let boil till it adheres to the spoon, stirring the whole time, rub through a tammie and put it into a clean stewpan, place over the fire, and when boiling add a gill of cream and two pats of butter; season with the juice of a lemon, a little salt and sugar if required; pour the sauce over the poulardes and cockscombs, glaze the tongue, truffles, and sweetbreads and serve immediately; do not pour the sauce over until quite ready to serve.

Poulardes à la Vicomtesse.

Make a croustade as represented in the plate   roast two poulardes in vegetables as in the last; place the croustade in the middle of the dish, and upon each gradation of it stick an attelet, upon which you have placed two plover's eggs warmed in stock; place the poulardes on the dish breast to breast, and at the tail of each lay three larded lambs' sweetbreads
make a border of mashed potatoes round, upon which dress slices of cooked ham warmed in stock, and cut in the shape of fillets of fowls; have ready prepared the following sauce: cut into thin slices a little carrot, turnip, onion, and celery, put them into a stewpan, with an ounce of butter, three cloves, half a blade of mace, a bay-leaf, a sprig of thyme and parsley, pass them over a brisk fire until lightly browned, add four tablespoonfuls of tarragon vinegar, and one ditto of common vinegar, let boil, add two quarts of brown sauce   and one of consommé, boil it twenty minutes, keeping it stirred, pass it through a tammie into a clean stewpan, add half a

pint of tomata sauce and two tablespoonfuls of red currant jelly; boil altogether till it adheres to the spoon, season with a little salt and pepper if required, sauce over the poulardes; glaze the pieces of ham and serve immediately.

Poulardes à la Jeanne d'Arc.

Roast the poulardes in vegetables as before, and dress them with croustade, garniture, and sauce as described in fillet of beef à la Jeanne d'Arc

Poulardes à la Jeune Princesse.

Bone two nice poulardes as for poularde à l'ambassadrice them on a cloth, have ready prepared four pounds of forcemeat spread some half an inch in thickness over the inside of the poulardes; have ready boiled a Russian tongue, which cut in halves lengthwise, trim each half, lay one upon the middle of each poularde, cut twelve pieces of fat bacon four inches in length and the thickness of your finger, lay three pieces upon each side of the tongue at equal distances apart, and between each piece lay rows of small very green gherkins, season with a little salt and pepper, cover with a little more of the forcemeat, roll and sew up the poulardes, tie them in cloths and braise two hours, as directed for poulardes à l'ambassadrice; when done take them out of the cloths, pull out the packthread you sewed them up with, dress them on your dish in a slanting direction, make a border of mashed potatoes round, have ready twenty small croustades de beurre à la purée de volaille which dress upon the mashed potatoes at equal distances apart, and upon the top of each place a plover's egg (from which you have peeled off all the shell) warmed in broth, between each croustade lay small bunches of asparagus (previously boiled), cut an inch and a half in length, and six or eight in a bunch; have ready the following sauce: put three quarts of white sauce

and one of white stock in a stewpan, the sauce strongly flavoured with mushrooms, place it over the fire, keep stirring, reduce to two-thirds, add a gill of whipped cream, season with a little salt and sugar if required; pour the sauce over the poulardes, and upon the breast of each sprinkle a few heads of sprue grass nicely boiled and cut very small; in carving they must be cut across, it will resemble marble.

Poulardes à la Financière.

Roast two poulardes in vegetables as usual; have ready boiled two ox tongues, trim them, nicely cutting off part of the tip; when the poulardes are done dress them up on your dish tail to tail, dress the two tongues crosswise, that is, the tips of the tongues touching the tails of the poulardes, have a very fine larded sweetbread nicely cooked and glazed, which place in the centre (this way of dishing them is very simple but very elegant); have ready the following ragout: put twenty dressed cockscombs, twenty heads of mushrooms, four truffles cut in slices, twelve pieces of sweetbread the size of half-crowns (well blanched), and twenty small quenelles in a stewpan, in another stewpan put two glasses of sherry, half an ounce of glaze, a little cayenne pepper, and a bay-leaf; reduce to half over a good fire, then add three quarts of espagnole or brown sauce and twenty spoonfuls of consommé boil and skim, reduce, keeping it stirred till it becomes a good demi-glace and adheres to the back of the spoon, pass it through a tammie into the stewpan containing the garniture, add a little powdered sugar, make all hot together, pour over and round the poulardes, glaze the tongues and serve.

Poulardes à la Warsovienne.

Roast two large poulardes in vegetables, and let them get cold, then take all the meat from the breast, but be careful to leave a rim half an inch in thickness, cut up the flesh in small dice, put it into a stewpan with fifteen spoonfuls of white sauce two truffles cut in slices, and twelve pieces of stewed cucumber season with a little sugar, salt, and a very little grated nutmeg; stir all very gently over the fire (being careful not to break the pieces of cucumber), when it boils add the yolks of two eggs mixed with two spoonfuls of cream, stir them in quickly; have ready warmed in stock the carcasses of the poulardes, place the mince in the breasts, egg over, and bread-crumb round the rims, place them in the oven twenty minutes to set, then dress them breast to breast on your dish; poach twelve plovers' eggs very nicely, lay six upon each poularde, that is, three upon each side of the breast to form a diamond, then place a small larded lamb's sweetbread upon the top between the two poulardes and in the centre of the eggs, place a fine cauliflower on each side, and sauce over with a sauce béchamel, or maître d'hôtel glaze the sweetbread and serve.

Poulardes aux légumes printaniers.

Roast two poulardes in vegetables as before, then with a sharp knife turn forty young carrots and forty young turnips, keeping them in their shape as much as possible, wash and place them in separate stewpans, with a pint of veal stock and half a teaspoonful of sugar, boil until the stock is reduced to glaze, by which time they will be well done, place them in a bain marie to keep hot, peel also forty young onions the same size as your turnips, butter a sauté-pan, put in half an ounce of sugar (sifted), over which place the onions, cover with veal stock and let them stew until the stock forms a thickish glaze, place them in the hot closet until wanted, then take up the poulardes, dress tail to tail on your dish, make a border of mashed potatoes round, and at each end place a fine head of cauliflower nicely boiled, then place alternately an onion and a turnip with a carrot upon the top between, making a pyramid in the middle of the border on each side; for sauce put the glaze from the vegetables and onions into a stewpan together, boil and skim off all the butter, add two quarts of brown sauce, reduce quickly, keeping it stirred all the time, until it adheres to the back of the spoon, add a little salt if required; pour the sauce over the whole and serve.

Poulardes aux légumes verts.

Roast the poulardes in vegetables as usual, then take ten large turnips, cut each in halves exactly in the centre, peel them thin without leaving the marks of the knife, and scoop out the centres to form them into cups, with a round cutter the size of half-a-crown-piece, cut twenty pieces of turnip one inch in thickness to form stands, stew them nicely in stock as in the last, but not too much done, and place them in the bain marie till ready to serve, then place a border of mashed potatoes round the interior of the dish, leaving sufficient room for your poulardes, and at each end stick a croustade of bread cut in cups but larger than those of turnips, place the turnip cups upon their stands at equal distances apart upon the mashed potatoes, place a nice head of cauliflower upon each croustade, have ready boiled some very young peas and heads of asparagus, fill the cups alternately with each, place your poulardes in the centre. and have ready the following sauce: put two quarts of white sauce   and a pint of white stock in a stewpan, with the glaze from the turnips, reduce to two-thirds, skim, season with a little salt and sugar, finish with a gill of cream, sauce all over, but lightly over the vegetables, and serve.

Capons may of course be dressed in the same manner as poulardes for removes, but to give a second series would only be a useless repetition.

Petits Poulets à la Warenzorf.

Procure four very nice spring chickens trussed as for boiling, roast them in vegetables, as described   have also ready boiled and nicely trimmed two deer tongues, place one at each end of the dish making the tips meet in the centre, place a chicken at each corner, its tail in the centre, and between each lay a bunch of fine boiled asparagus; you have made a round fluted croustade of bread about four inches high, and the same in diameter, ornament it on the top with rings the size of a shilling, fried very white, and scoop out the middle of the croustade to form a cup; place it in the centre of your dish, with some fine heads of asparagus cut about four inches in length standing upright in it, glaze the tongues nicely, have two quarts of sauce purée d'asperges   ready, which pour over the chickens and serve very hot.

Petits Poulets à la Périgord à blanc.

Scrape four ounces of fat bacon, which put into a stewpan, with two bay-leaves, three cloves, and a blade of mace, set over the fire to melt, and when quite hot take out the spice and bay-leaves, add ten large truffles cut in slices, and four chopped very fine, with a quart of white sauce
place it over the fire to reduce, keeping it stirred until becoming very thick, finish with two yolks of eggs and place it on a dish to cool; procure four nice spring chickens, detach the skin from the breasts without breaking, force the above preparation under the skins, sew the skin down (but not too tight, or it would burst in roasting), roast them in vegetables as usual; have ready a croustade in the form of a vase, which place in the centre of your dish filled with fine truffles warmed in strong stock, dress the chickens with taste around it, first draining them upon a cloth, glaze lightly, and have ready the following sauce: put two quarts of white sauce   into a stewpan, with a pint of good veal broth, place it on the fire and when boiling add six large French truffles cut in thin slices, and half a teaspoonful of sugar, reduce, keeping it stirred until becoming thickish, add half a gill of whipped cream; pour the sauce round the chickens and serve very hot.

Petits Poulets à la Macédoine de légumes.

Procure four spring chickens, roast them in vegetables, but just before they are done take off all the paper and vegetables and let them get a nice gold colour; prepare and poach a piece of forcemeat four inches square, and another two inches square, place the smaller one upon the larger in the centre of the dish, dress the chickens by placing the tails upon the forcemeat and the breasts towards the edges of the dish; you have previously peeled and turned twelve Jerusalem artichokes in the shape of pears, and stewed in white stock, place three at the breast of each chicken, and a piece of boiled cauliflower between each at the tail, build some Brussels sprouts pyramidically at the top, and sauce with macédoine de légumes à brun

Fowls may be dressed in the same manner as the chickens and are used when chickens cannot be obtained.

Petits Poulets à l'Indienne.

Put one pound of rice nicely boiled in a basin with a quarter of a pound of suet, a little pepper, salt, cayenne, grated nutmeg, chopped parsley, two spoonfuls of bread-crumbs, one of currie powder, and three or four eggs, mix all well together, then have four spring chickens untrussed, fill them with the above, and truss them as for boiling, stew them one hour gently in a braise make a round croustade of the form of a cup, five inches high, fill with some beautiful white rice in pyramid, with seven or eight mild Indian pickles interspersed, dress the chickens round the croustade, with a piece of boiled bacon three inches long and two broad between each, pour about two quarts of sauce à l'Indienne
and serve very hot.

Petits Poulets au jus d'estragon.

Roast three spring chickens in vegetables, the same as for petits poulets à la macédoine de légumes, dress them on your dish, and pour a sauce au jus d'estragon

Petits Poulets à la Marie Stuart.

Procure four spring chickens trussed as for boiling, detach carefully part of the skin from the breasts, and lay slices of French truffles under the skin, shaping a heart upon the breasts of each, prepare half a pound of maître d'hôtel butter divide it in four parts, and place one on the top of the truffles under the skin of each breast, covering with the skin, then put half a pound of butter, two onions, two bay-leaves, and two wine-glasses of pale brandy, with a little stock into a flat stewpan, lay in the chickens, place a sheet of buttered paper over, put on the cover, place it ten minutes over a sharp fire, then set in a moderate oven for an hour, when done take out the string, lay them on a clean cloth to drain; have ready a croustade in the form of a pyramid, which place in the centre of your dish entirely enveloped with mashed potatoes half an inch in thickness; have ready some fine heads of asparagus boiled very green, and cut about an inch in length, stick them upon the pyramid with a small nice white head of cauliflower at the top, dish your chickens round and sauce with a thin purée of truffles round them.

Petits Poussins à la Chanoinaise.

Have ready three parts roasted in vegetables six very young spring chickens trussed as for boiling, cover them all over with forcemeat throw some chopped truffles and ham lightly over, and pat them into a flat stewpan just covered with some good veal stock, set them in a moderate oven twenty minutes, with the cover over, and when done dress them at the corners of the dish upon a little mashed potatoes, place a small croustade in the centre, upon which place a nicely-cooked larded sweetbread, glaze well, and have ready the following sauce: put two quarts of demi-glace into a stewpan, with a little sugar, and when boiling have ready a tongue (ready boiled) cut in slices the size of half-a-crown-piece, and six large truffles also sliced, put them into the sauce, and when very hot pour into your dish, but not over the chickens; serve very hot.

Petits Poulets à la Printaniere.

Roast four spring chickens in vegetables, have ready some young carrots, turnips, and onions, stewed as directed make a small border of mashed potatoes round the dish, dress the vegetables with taste upon it, variegating them with peas or asparagus heads boiled very green, dress the chickens in the centre and have ready the following sauce: put two quarts of demi-glace into a stewpan, reduce well over the fire, keeping it stirred, add half a teaspoonful of sugar and the glaze from the vegetables, reduce again till it adheres to the back of the spoon, pour over the chickens and vegetables, and serve very hot.

Petits Poussins à la Tartare.

Procure four very young spring chickens, not trussed, cut off the feet below the joints, break the bone in each leg, then cut an incision in the thigh of the chicken and turn the legs into it, cut the chickens open down the back-bone, and beat them flat, fry five minutes in butter in a sauté-pan, season with a little pepper and salt, egg and bread-crumb them all over, lay them on a gridiron over a moderate fire, and broil a nice light-brown colour; for sauce put ten tablespoonfuls of white sauce and six of consommé in a stewpan, and when it has boiled ten minutes add ten spoonfuls of sauce tartare stir altogether till quite hot, but do not let it boil, pour it on your dish, garnish the edges of the dish with slices of Indian pickle, dress the chickens upon the sauce and serve directly; the sauce tartare may also be served cold with the chickens glazed and served hot upon it.

Petits Poussins à la Maréchal.

Truss and broil four chickens precisely as in the last, and have ready the following sauce: put three tablespoonfuls of tarragon vinegar into a stewpan, with a small piece of glaze, half a pint of brown sauce and twenty tablespoonfuls of consommé reduce ten minutes until forming a demi-glace, pour the sauce in the dish, glaze the chickens, dish them upon the sauce and serve.

Goose à la Chipolata.

Truss your goose nicely, and lard the breast (with lardons of fat bacon three inches long) here and there slantwise, then proceed exactly as for turkey à la chipolata

Goose stuffed with chesnuts.

Procure a fine goose, truss it, chop the liver very fine, cut an onion in small dice, put them in a stewpan, with the liver, and a quarter of a pound of scraped fat bacon, pass them over a slow fire for ten minutes or a little longer, have ready roasted and peeled thirty fine chesnuts, put them in the stewpan, with two bay-leaves, let them stew slowly over the fire half an hour, season with pepper, salt, and sugar, and when nearly cold stuff the inside of the goose, which sew up at both ends; roast an hour and a half in vegetables, and just before it is done take away the paper and vegetables and let it get a nice light-brown colour, dress on a dish and serve a sauce au jus de tomates   in which you have introduced two tablespoonfuls of apple jelly; a little sage may be added to the above preparation if approved of.

Goose à la Portugaise.

Prepare your goose, then peel four Portugal onions, cut them in thin slices and put them into a stewpan with a quarter of a pound of butter; let them simmer over a slow fire until quite tender, then add a tablespoonful of flour, a little pepper, salt, grated nutmeg, and sugar, with half a pint of white sauce   boil altogether twenty minutes, then stir in the yolks of two eggs and put it out on a dish to cool, stuff the goose with it, which roast as in the last, dress upon your dish with ten stewed Portugal onions and sauce as directed for stewed rump of beef à la Portugaise

Ducklings aux olives.

Roast four small ducklings in vegetables; have ready a croustade cut in the shape of a vase, set it on a few mashed potatoes in the centre of the dish, dress the ducklings with their tails towards it, and have ready the following sauce: put two quarts of demi-glace   in a stewpan, when it boils have ready turned sixty French olives, which throw into it, season with half a tablespoonful of sugar, when very hot put the olives on the top of the croustade, pour the sauce over and serve directly.

Ducklings au jus d'orange.

Roast four ducklings as in the previous article, dress a croustade in the centre of the dish, upon which place a fine Seville orange with a silver attelet through it, dress the ducklings round, and serve with a jus d'orange sauce

Ducklings aux légumes printaniers.

Roast them as above, and serve as directed for the poulardes (No. 521).

Ducklings à la Chartre.

Roast your ducklings as before, have ready fifty young turnips turned in the shape of pears, put half an ounce of sifted sugar into a convenient-sized stewpan, set over the fire, and when it melts and assumes a brownish tinge add half a pound of butter and the turnips, toss them over every now and then, and when about three parts done and a light-brown colour turn them out on a cloth to drain the butter from them, likewise drain all the butter from the stewpan, put your turnips again into it, with a quart of brown sauce half a pint of white stock, and a bunch of parsley, boil altogether ten minutes, or till the sauce adheres to the spoon, dress a croustade in the form of a vase in the centre of the dish, dress the ducklings round, take the parsley from the sauce, dress some of the turnips with taste upon the croustade and the remainder between each duckling; pour the sauce round and serve.

Haunch of Venison.

May be decidedly called the second great pedestal; turtle soup and haunch of venison certainly being the two great pedestals, or Gog and Magog of English cookery. It is appreciated from the independent citizen to the throne; for where is there a citizen of taste, a man of wealth, or a gourmet, who does not pay due homage to this delicious and recherché joint, which ever has and ever will be in vogue; but even after all that nature has done in point of flavour, should it fall into the hands of some inexperienced person to dress, and be too much done, its appearance and flavour would be entirely spoilt, its delicious and delicate fat melted, and the gravy lost; of the two it would be preferred underdone, but that is very bad and hardly excusable, when it requires nothing but attention to serve this glorious dish in perfection.

A good haunch of venison weighing from about twenty to twenty-five pounds will take from three to four hours roasting before a good solid fire; trim the haunch by cutting off part of the knuckle and sawing off the chine bone, fold the flap over, then envelope it in a flour and water paste rather stiff, and an inch thick, tie it up in strong paper, four sheets in thickness, place it in your cradle spit so that it will turn quite even, place it at first very close to the fire until the paste is well crusted, pouring a few ladlefuls of hot dripping over occasionally to prevent the paper catching fire, then put it rather further from the fire, which must be quite clear, solid, and have sufficient frontage to throw the same heat on every part of the venison; when it has roasted the above time take it up, remove it from the paste and paper, run a thin skewer into the thickest part to ascertain if done, if it resists the skewer it is not done, and must be tied up and put down again, but if the fire is good that time will sufficiently cook it, glaze the top well, salamander until a little brown, put a frill upon the knuckle, and serve very hot with plenty of plain boiled French beans separate. For the mode of carving a haunch of venison, see preface.

Haunch of Doe Venison à la Corinthienne.

Trim your haunch and lard the fillet of the loin and the leg as you would a fricandeau, put it for a week in a marinade turning it over every other day; place it on a spit, tied up in oiled paper, and roast it two hours, but just before taking up, take off all the paper, to give a nice colour; dress it on your dish with a frill at the knuckle, and have ready the following sauce: well wash and pick half a pound of fine currants, soak them in water two hours, dry them well on a sieve, put half a pint of the marinade through a sieve into a stewpan, with two glasses of port wine, and two chopped eschalots, reduce to half, add a quart of brown sauce reduce till it adheres to the back of the spoon, add a tablespoonful of currant jelly, pass it through a tammie into another stewpan, add your currants, season with a little cayenne pepper, and salt if required, pour the sauce round the haunch, and serve.

Necks of Doe Venison à la Corinthienne.

Trim two necks of venison by cutting out the shoulders, not too deep, cut the breast off rather narrow, slip your knife between the rib bones and the flesh to half way up, saw off the bones, skewer the flap over, detach the chine bones from the flesh, saw them off, and lard the fillets; put them in marinade one day (they must be well covered), tie them up in oiled paper, and roast for one hour; when done glaze and salamander the tops, dress them fillet to fillet on your dish, and sauce the same as for haunch à la Corinthienne.

Faisans à la Corsaire.

Procure three young pheasants, truss them as for boiling, chop the livers very fine, and put them into a basin with a quarter of a pound of chopped suet, one pound of bread-crumbs, a little pepper, salt, grated nutmeg, chopped parsley, and thyme; mix the whole well together with four eggs, put in a mortar, pound it well, stuff the birds with it, and roast them in vegetables; make a croustade shaped like the bows of a ship, dress it at the head of the dish, make a large quenelle which ornament with truffles to fancy; run a silver attelet through it lengthwise, and stick it at the top of the croustade, dress the pheasants on the dish, the tails of two of them touching the croustade, and the other between, with its breast towards the end of the dish; have ready the following sauce: put two quarts of the sauce à l'essence de gibier in a stewpan, with half a pint of white broth; reduce till it adheres to the spoon, then add twenty dressed cockscombs and twenty heads of mushrooms; sauce over the pheasants and serve.

Faisans à la Garde Chasse.

Procure four very young hen pheasants, truss them for roasting, merely cut off the tips of the claws, make a small incision in the leg at the knuckles, and truss them with their claws resting on their thighs, and their knuckles over their tails; stuff them with the same preparation as in the last, but adding a glass of brandy and half a gill of double cream; put them on your spit, have ready washed and cut from the roots a few good handfuls of heather from the mountain, surround the birds with it, and tie them in oiled paper; roast them three quarters of an hour, take them up, and dress them on your dish in the form of a cross; have four large quenelles of game and place one between each pheasant; have ready the following sauce: put two glasses of port wine in a stewpan, with a teaspoonful of sugar, and an ounce of glaze; boil three minutes, then add a quart of the sauce à l'essence de gibier boil altogether ten minutes, skim, add two ounces of fresh butter, stir it in with a wooden spoon; when quite melted pour the sauce over the birds, and serve.

Faisans truffés à la Piémontaise.

Procure four young pheasants as above, but they must be quite fresh, stuff the breasts of them with half a pound of truffles prepared as for poularde à la Périgord only using half oil and half bacon, and adding half a clove of garlic scraped; show as much truffles as possible under the skin; they must be kept in that way a week or more (according to the weather), before they are fit for dressing; roast nearly an hour in oiled paper of a light gold colour, dress upon your dish in the form of a cross, have ready the following sauce: put two quarts of clear aspic in a stewpan, reduce twenty minutes, cut six raw or preserved truffles in slices, put them into the aspic with a glass of champagne, hock, or madeira, and a little sugar; stew them twenty minutes, sauce over your birds, and serve very hot.

Faisans à l'Extravagante.

This is a very elegant remove, and can be made where woodcocks are plentiful, but to the economiser it would appear a most extravagant extravaganza; procure two large pheasants and six woodcocks, fillet the woodcocks and cut each fillet in halves lengthwise, put two ounces of scraped bacon in a sautépan with a tablespoonful of chopped eschalots and half a pottle of chopped mushrooms; lay the fillets over them, season with pepper and salt, set them over the fire five minutes, turn the fillets, set them again on the fire five minutes longer, add twenty tablespoonfuls of bechamel sauce half a pound of cockscombs previously cooked, a little grated nutmeg, and half a spoonful of sugar; it must be rather highly seasoned; add three yolks of eggs, stir a minute over the fire till the egg sets, then put it on a dish to cool; when firm divide it in two, and stuff the pheasants with it, having previously extracted all the breast bone, sew the skin of the neck over on the back, but do not draw it too tight, or it would burst on the breast; surround with fat bacon, and tie them in oiled paper; roast them one hour, but just before they are done take off the paper and bacon; shake flour over, and they will become brown and crisp; have ready prepared the following sauce: put the remainder of the woodcocks in a stewpan, with two glasses of sherry, a pint of white stock, two eschalots (cut in slices), a little parsley, thyme, and bay-leaf, two cloves, and half a blade of mace, let simmer a quarter of an hour, add a quart of brown sauce, let the whole boil together twenty minutes at the corner of the stove, take out the pieces of woodcock, and pass the sauce through a tammie into a clean stewpan, take the flesh and trails of the woodcocks from the bones, which pound well in the mortar, then put it in the sauce, boil it up again, season with a little pepper, salt, and half a teaspoonful of sugar, and rub it through a tammie with two wooden spoons, the sauce is then ready; for garniture cut twenty-four pieces of bread in the form of hearts, cover them on one side with forcemeat rather thick in the middle, and fix a cockscomb ready dressed upon each; butter a sauté-pan, and lay them in it; cover them over with a sheet of buttered paper, and place them half an hour in a moderate oven; make a border of forcemeat poached in pieces an inch broad and half an inch thick, which lay on your dish, upon which dress them, place the pheasants in the centre, pour the sauce round, glaze the birds and cockscombs, and serve.

The way to carve pheasants dressed this way is as follows: the breast being free from bone, detach the legs with a knife, and cut the breast in slices in a slanting direction; the scraped bacon will escape in roasting, keeping the birds moist; they will not cut greasy, but will have a marbled appearance like gallantine.

Grouse à la Rob Roy.

Grouse are the most favourite birds in this country, and certainly the most welcome; they make their first appearance on the 12th of August, a time when most delicate palates are fatigued with domestic volatile productions, at that period they are very properly used for roasts only; but when more plentiful they are very excellent dressed in the manners I have here described, though seldom or ever used for removes; I have, for the sake of variety which is said to be charming, given a few new methods. Pick, draw, and truss four grouse, make a stuffing like for the pheasants using the liver of the grouse, stuff and place them on the spit, surrounded with fat bacon and sprigs of heather, moistened with a glass of whiskey, tie them up in paper and roast three quarters of an hour, dress on a dish in the form of a cross, and have ready the following sauce: put a quart of good melted butter in a stewpan on the fire, and just as it begins to boil, add a quarter of a pound of butter; stir the sauce till the butter is melted, season rather high, and pour over your birds; (the sauce must be rather thick, but not too thick;) under each bird place a piece of toasted bread well glazed; serve very hot.

Grouse à la Garde Chasse.

Of Black Cocks and Grey Hens.

These birds are a similar flavour to the grouse, only much larger, and may be dressed just in the same manner, only two cocks will be sufficient for a remove of ten or twelve persons if well garnished with quenelles, cockscombs, mushrooms, truffles, &c.

Hare à la Macgregor.

Skin a fine young hare, and truss it as for roasting, stuff with a forcemeat made of the liver   put it on the spit, rub well with oil, and while roasting sprinkle a little flour over now and then; have ready the fillets of three other hares skinned and nicely larded, put some butter in a sauté-pan, and fry them gently of light brown colour, rather underdone; cut each fillet in halves, and have twelve pieces of toasted bread cut in the form of hearts, of the same size as the fillets; dress them alternately on your dish upon a border of mashed potatoes, dress the hare in the centre, glaze the fillets and bread, and pour a quart of sauce poivrade (No. 33), in which you have introduced a spoonful of mild orange marmalade instead of the currant jelly, over the hare, and serve very hot.

Levraut à la Coursière.

Skin and draw two leverets just caught by the dogs, save the blood in a basin, truss them for roasting, lard the fillets, roast half an hour before a quick fire, put a quart of poivrade sauce   in a stewpan; when boiling stir quickly with a wooden spoon, and pour in the blood; add a little salt, cayenne pepper, a tablespoonful of currant jelly, four pats of butter, and the juice of a lemon; sauce over the leverets and serve immediately.

FLANCS.

Flancs are required in every dinner where there are more than four entrées; they are served upon oval dishes of from eighteen inches in length to nine in width, and require a little depth; for flancs being made dishes, like removes, the dish must contain the sauce. My readers will perceive by the Index that many of them are like the removes; but these I shall merely give references to, my object in placing them with the flancs being to show that by being reduced in size they will do for flancs in large dinners, and also be an assistance in the making of bills of fare.

Flancs are to be made of one or two solid pieces of poultry, game, butcher's meat, or pastry, and keep everything which is divided into many pieces, as cotelettes, fillets, escalopes, fricassées, salmis, &c., for entrées as much as possible, by doing which you will add more importance to your dinner, and cause more harmony in the arrangement.

Fillet of Beef piqué aux légumes printaniers.

Procure a piece of fillet of beef fifteen inches in length, lard, trim, and dress it as directed when ready to serve dress a border of mashed potatoes on your dish; have ready twenty young carrots, twenty young turnips, with twenty small onions, dressed as directed for poulardes dish them upon the mashed potatoes with a small cauliflower nicely boiled at each end of the dish, place your fillet in the centre, glaze it, and sauce with a demi-glace, made also as directed for the poulardes, but half the quantity will be sufficient.

Filet de Bœuf au jus de groseilles.

Procure and lard a piece of fillet of beef the same size as in the last, pickle it four or five days, as directed for filet de bœuf when wanted take it from the marinade, dry it, and roast it in paper, but ten minutes before it is done take off the paper to allow it to colour a little; place it on your dish, and have ready the following sauce: run half a pint of the marinade through a sieve into a stewpan, add an ounce of glaze, place it on the fire, reduce it to half, add a quart of brown sauce, and again reduce it till it becomes a clear demi-glace; skim it when required, add half the rind of a lemon, the peelings of a few mushrooms, a little scraped garlic, the size of a pea, and a spoonful of very bright currant jelly; stir it two minutes over the fire, season it rather high, pass it through a tammie, sauce over the fillet, and serve.

Fillet of Beef à la Beyrout.

Procure but a piece of fillet the same size as in the last, and proceed as directed

For Filet de Bœuf à la Milanaise,
Do. au jus d'orange, and
Do. au jus de tomates,

merely substituting a piece of the fillet when serving them as flancs.

Langue de Bœuf à la Marquise.

Boil a nice ox-tongue three hours, when done take the skin off carefully; by allowing it to get cold, you can cut any design upon it your fancy may dictate, but I prefer sending them plain, merely trimming it. You have previously filleted and dressed three chickens, as described for suprême de volaille, of mashed potatoes round your dish, and dress half the fillets of chicken on each side, one upon the other in a slanting direction; have ready dressed four nice larded sweetbreads, place two at each end, and the tongue in the centre, have ready the following sauce: put a pint and a half of white sauce in the sauté-pan in which you cooked your fillets of chickens, with twelve spoonfuls of good veal stock, stir it over the fire till it becomes rather thick, then add a gill of cream and a little powdered sugar, mix all well together, pass it through a tammie into a stewpan when hot, sauce over the fillets, glaze the sweetbreads and tongue, and serve very hot.

Langue de Bœuf à la Prima Donna.

Boil the tongue as in the last, then have ready twenty-four quenelles of veal dress a low border of mashed potatoes round the dish, upon which dress the quenelles, making them go quite round, then have ready the following sauce: put twenty spoonfuls of white sauce and ten of veal stock in a stewpan; let it boil ten minutes, then add a quarter of a pound of maître d'hôtel butter mix it very quick over the fire, and when melted sauce over the quenelles; put a nicely boiled Brussels sprout between each quenelle, glaze the tongue, and serve.

Langue de Bœuf à la St. Aulaire.

Cook the tongue as before, and when done fix it on the dish upon mashed potatoes; have ready the following ragout: cut four middling-sized cucumbers into pieces about an inch and a half in length, split each piece in three, take out the seeds from each piece, peel them and trim them at the corners, put them in a stewpan with an ounce of butter, half a spoonful of powdered sugar, and two chopped eschalots; stew the cucumbers very gently till quite tender, but not to break them, then cut the breast of a cooked fowl into slices the size of the pieces of cucumber and add with them; then add a quart of hot bechamel sauce and a little white stock, shake the stewpan over the fire, but do not stir it with a spoon, or you would break the contents; finish with a liaison made from the yolk of one egg, pour it round the tongue, and serve.

Langue de Bœuf à la Jardinière.

Cook the tongue as before, fix it in your dish upon mashed potatoes, and serve with a jardiniere sauce round it.

Langue de Bœuf à la Milanaise.

Cook as before, and serve with a sauce à la Milanaise under it, to which has been added some fillets of fowl cut the same size as the pieces of macaroni.

Ox-tongues may also be served with sauce piquante or sauce à l'Italienne and they are frequently served as a flanc, quite plain, especially when the opposite flanc is composed of veal or poultry.

Westphalia Ham, small.

These hams require to be well soaked in water, and scraped previous to dressing; boil from three to four hours, and when done take off the skin, leaving a little on the knuckle, which you cut as fancy may direct; glaze it nicely, put a paper frill upon the knuckle-bone, and serve it plain, or it may be served with any of the following sauces: poivrade jardinière Milanaise or dressed spinach but when it is intended to be eaten with a remove of poultry, it is as well served plain.

Loin of Veal à la Crèmière.

Procure part of a loin about the size your dish will conveniently hold, place it on a spit and have ready some vegetables of all kinds cut small; lay them on two or three sheets of thickish paper, moisten them with half a pint of cream, tie the veal up in them and roast it two hours, make a border of mashed potatoes round your dish, upon which dress twelve nice poached eggs; take up the veal, clear it from the vegetables, and dress it in the centre; have ready the following sauce: put a quart of bechamel sauce

in a stewpan, with a little grated nutmeg, salt, and sugar; stir it over a quick fire, boil it ten minutes, then add a gill of cream, the juice of a lemon, and an ounce of fresh butter, pour it over the eggs and veal, and serve; the sauce requires to be rather thick, but if too much so, thin it with a little milk; if sprue grass is in season, a few of the heads boiled, and lard between the eggs, would have a pleasing effect.

> For Loins à la purée de céleri,
>   Do. macédoine de légumes, and
>   Do. à la Strasbourgienne

Noix de veau pique au jus.

Procure a very white leg of veal from a cow calf, saw off the knuckle, lay the fillet on the table and cut it open without cutting through the meat, that is cut from the bone in the centre under the udder until you cut through the skin, take out the bone, and lay it out, there will be three separate lumps of meat, the largest of which is the noix (or nut); to cut it out press your hand upon it and with a sharp knife cut down close to the skin, separating it from the skin till it comes to the udder, then bring the knife up, lay the piece upon the table the best side downwards and beat it well, trim it of a nice shape, and lard it with pieces of fat bacon two inches long and slender in proportion, cut off the udder and sew it to the side, put a few slices of bacon in a flat stewpan, with two or three onions cut in slices, half a bunch of parsley, two bay-leaves, and a sprig of thyme, lay in the noix, add a pint of white broth, then put the lid on the stewpan, and place it in a moderate oven for three hours, occasionally looking at it, taking care that the gravy does not become dry or burnt, if it becomes dry add a little water to moisten it, but not enough to cover the veal, which moisten now and then with the gravy; when done, glaze it nicely, slightly colour it with the salamander if required, and lay it on a dish, keep it hot, then pass the gravy through a tammie into a smaller stewpan, set it on the corner of the fire, skim off all the fat, pour it in your dish, and lay the noix in the last moment of serving, or the fat would run, and give the gravy a bad appearance.

Noix de Veau à la Potagère.

Procure and dress a noix de veau as in the last, excepting the udder, which is not required, and you need not be particular about its being the leg of a cow calf; when cooked make a border of mashed potatoes round your dish, upon which dress several pieces of nice cauliflowers, (about the size of eggs,) which you have previously boiled, place the noix in the centre the last thing before serving, and have ready the following sauce: put thirty spoonfuls of white sauce in a stewpan with ten of the gravy from the noix, (free from fat,) boil ten minutes, then add half a gill of cream and a little sugar, pour the sauce over the cauliflowers, glaze the noix and serve immediately, throwing a few green peas, well boiled, round.

Noix de Veau à la Palestine.

Prepare and dress the noix as in the last, then wash and peel two dozen middling-sized Jerusalem artichokes, give them the shape of pears, boil them in salt and water in which you have put a piece of butter, boil them till tender, make a small border of mashed potatoes upon your dish, on which dress the artichokes, the thick part uppermost, scoop a piece out of the top of each, and stick in a nicely-boiled Brussels sprout, place the noix in the centre, glaze it and pour a thin sauce à la purée d'artichaut over the artichokes and serve.

Noix de Veau aux légumes nouveaux.

Prepare and dress the noix as in the last, then have prepared twenty young carrots, twenty young turnips, and twenty young onions, prepared as described in the article stewed rump of beef à la Flamande dress them tastefully upon your dish upon a thin border of mashed potatoes, place the noix in the centre and have ready the following sauce: mix the glaze from the vegetables with a quart of brown sauce and half a pint of the gravy from the noix, (but quite free from fat,) in a stewpan, place it over the fire and reduce till it becomes a thickish demi-glace, keeping it well skimmed, sauce over the vegetables, glaze the noix and serve.

Noix de Veau à la purée de champignons.

Prepare and dress the noix as before, and have ready a sauce à la purée de champignons   pour it on your dish, lay the noix over, glaze and serve immediately.

Noix de veau à la Prince Albert.

Prepare and dress the noix as before, have likewise ten lambs' sweetbreads larded and dressed   also ten plovers' eggs, which peel and warm in white stock, make a thin border of mashed potatoes round your dish, and dress the sweetbreads and plovers' eggs alternately upon it; place the noix in the centre, place a ring of truffles upon each plover's egg, and have ready the following sauce: pass the gravy from the noix and sweetbreads through a sieve into a stewpan, set it on the fire, skim off all the fat, add a quart of brown sauce   and a pint of consommé   reduce it quickly over the fire, keeping it stirred with a wooden spoon, and when reduced to a thinnish glaze take it off the fire, add a little sugar, and two pats of butter; glaze the sweetbreads and noix, sauce round and serve immediately.

Neck of Veal à la St. Clair.

Trim the best end of a very nice neck of veal, see Removes   roast it in vegetables, and give it a nice gold colour; make a border of mashed potatoes round your dish, upon which dress a number of slices of fried ham, (each cut in the shape of a long heart,) to form a crown, place the veal in the centre, and pour some very thin tomata sauce   (in which you have mixed half an ounce of anchovy butter) round, and serve. For neck of veal à la purée de celeri, ditto à la macédoine de légumes, and ditto à la crèmière,

Calf's Head à la Constantine.

Cook half a calf's head as directed   and when done lay it on a dish with another dish upon it, on which place a fourteen pounds weight, when cold cut twelve nice oval pieces out of it, egg each piece over with a paste-brush, and throw it into bread-crumbs mixed with chopped lean ham;

set them in the oven and when quite hot and of a nice gold colour dress them in a crown round your dish upon a border of mashed potatoes, place the brains at each end of the dish, and have ready the following sauce: make a quart of sauce au jus d'échalotte well seasoned, add to it twenty pickled mushrooms and forty very small white pickled onions, warm them five minutes in the sauce, then pour the sauce in the centre, glaze the pieces of calf's head and serve very hot. For calf's head en tortue, ditto à la Hollandaise, and ditto à l'amiral

Neck of Mutton demi Provençale.

Prepare and braise a neck of mutton as described for the Removes, see that it is not too fat; you have prepared a purée of onions like for the cotelettes spread some over the neck about a quarter of an inch thick, egg and bread-crumb it lightly, then put it in a hot oven twenty minutes, if not sufficiently coloured pass the salamander over it, then have ready the following sauce: put a pint of brown sauce in a stewpan, with half the quantity of good stock, reduce it over the fire till it comes to a nice demi-glace, add a little scraped garlic the size of a couple of peas, dress the neck in a dish and pour the sauce over; serve very hot; a little seasoning may be added to the sauce if required.

Neck of Mutton à la Soubise.

Prepare, lard, and braise a neck of mutton as described in the Removes when done glaze it well, pass the salamander over, place it in your dish, and serve with a sauce Soubise

Neck of Mutton à l'Algérienne.

Procure a large neck of mutton, trim it as before, and lard the lean part with fine cut bacon, like for the noix de veau, make two quarts of marinade and lay the neck in it for three days, then run a skewer through it and fix it on your spit, roast it about an hour, giving it a very good colour; have ready the following sauce: strain half a pint of the marinade into a stewpan, add a pint of brown sauce and a small piece of glaze, reduce it till forming a thickish demi-glace; you have previously soaked twenty very nice French plums in boiling water twenty minutes, drain them on a sieve, and when dry throw them into the sauce, season with a little salt and cayenne pepper, pour the sauce in your dish, dress the neck upon it and serve.

Neck of Mutton à la Portugaise.

Prepare, lard, and braise a neck of mutton as before, then peel six middling-sized Portugal onions, blanch them twenty minutes in boiling water, then lay them on a cloth to drain, put a quarter of a pound of butter in a flat stewpan, let it melt, lay in the onions, add one ounce of sugar, and a little salt, and just cover them with a little white stock, let them simmer gently for one hour or more until quite tender, take them out carefully, lay on a cloth, cut them in halves, dress in a border round the dish, and lay the neck in the centre, then take the butter from the stock the onions were stewed in, put half a pint of it in a stewpan, with a quart of white sauce

and half a pint of stock, reduce it till it becomes again thickish, and pour it over the onions round the mutton, which glaze and serve very hot.

For neck of mutton à la légumière, ditto à la Brétonne, and ditto à la Chartre

Loin of Mutton en Carbonade.

Bone a loin of mutton carefully, leaving the small fillet attached, lard it well with pieces of lean ham and fat bacon, season with chopped eschalots, chopped parsley, pepper and salt, roll it up as tight as possible, previously putting in some forcemeat   tie it up with string, put in a stewpan, with some white stock and vegetables, let it stew gently two hours and a half, then take it up, cut off the string, trim it at each end, glaze the top, pass the salamander over to give it a nice colour, and serve with dressed spinach

Carbonade de Mouton à la Bourginotte.

Prepare a loin of mutton as in the last, then peel one hundred button onions, put half an ounce of pounded sugar in a stewpan, set it over the fire and as soon as it is melted add half an ounce of butter and the onions, place them over a slow fire, tossing them every now and then, when getting tender add a pint and a half of white sauce   and a pint of white stock, with a small bunch of parsley, thyme, and bay-leaf, set it on the fire till the onions are quite done, take them out with a colander spoon and put them in a clean stewpan, reduce the sauce till it becomes rather thickish, pass it through a tammie upon the onions, warm altogether, pour the sauce in your dish, place the carbonade in the centre, which glaze and serve very hot.

www.ingramcontent.com/pod-product-compliance
Lightning Source LLC
Chambersburg PA
CBHW081730100526
44591CB00016B/2564